30 Heirloom Projects with Complete How-to-Knit Instructions

KNITTING FOR BABY

melanie falick & kristin nicholas

photographs by ross whitaker

STC CRAFT | A MELANIE FALICK BOOK | NEW YORK

FOR BEN AND JULIA

Published in 2008 by Stewart, Tabori & Chang
An imprint of Harry N. Abrams, Inc.

Originally published in hardcover in 2002 by Stewart, Tabori & Chang

Text copyright © 2002 Melanie Falick and Kristin Nicholas
Illustrations copyright © 2002 Kristin Nicholas
Photographs copyright © 2002 Ross Whitaker
Photographs on pages 6–7, 10–11, 26–27, 38–39, 50–51, 66–67, 114–115, 140–141
© 2002 David Hughes/Hotfoot Studio
Design © 2002 Lynne Yeamans and Christine Licata

Library of Congress Cataloging-in-Publication Data

Falick, Melanie
    Knitting for baby : 30 heirloom projects with complete how-to-knit instructions/
Melanie Falick & Kristin Nicholas ; photographs by Ross Whitaker.
        p. cm.
    Includes index.
    ISBN 978-1-58479-680-0
        1. Knitting--Patterns. 2. Infants' clothing. 3. Soft toy making. I. Nicholas, Kristin. II.
Title.

TT825 .F35 2002
746.43'20432--dc21

2001058527

Cover Designer: Alissa Faden
Production Manager: Jacqueline Poirier

The text of this book was composed in Sabon and Engravers Gothic.

Printed in China
10 9 8 7 6 5 4 3 2 1

harry n. abrams, inc.
a subsidiary of La Martinière Groupe
115 West 18th Street
New York, NY 10011
www.abramsbooks.com

CONTENTS

INTRODUCTION

Knitting for a baby is a gesture of love. It is a prayer, a meditation. As we form each stitch, we express with our fingers our dreams and hopes for the baby's health and happiness. If we are knitting while pregnant, it is a way of connecting with the baby inside. If we are knitting for the baby of a friend or family member, it is a way of sharing in their joy. When babies wear what we have made for them they are wrapped in our love—safe, warm, and protected.

Both of us have been knitting for a long time. We've taught many people to knit, and we've knit for a lot of babies, including our own. Through the years, we have watched over and over as women (and, occasionally, men) have come to the idea of knitting for a baby—sometimes as lapsed knitters, sometimes as complete beginners. We've even noticed that when we teach children to knit, as soon as many of them begin to grasp the knit stitch, they start to talk with excitement about the projects they want to make for the babies in their lives—often family members or the babies of school teachers or of neighbors. Sometimes their plans are realized, sometimes not, but their intentions are always generous and loving. The impulse to knit for little ones seems almost innate.

While in early history knitting was a necessary means of clothing children and adults, in most parts of the world we now come to it as a personal choice. When we choose to knit for a baby, we are treating ourselves and the recip-ient to something unique and special in a world in which the work of the hand is increasingly rare. If the project is well cared for, it can be shared by many. It is possible that one day long from now it will be admired by the grownup for whom it was originally made or the newest parents to inherit it for their baby—and, like an old photograph, it will make them feel close to the maker as well as to the people whose lives it has already touched.

We created this book in hopes of teaching new knitters, inspiring knitters whose skills may be rusty, and satisfying experienced, active knitters. We present projects from the most basic up to the intermediate level, all with explicit instructions in easy-to-understand language. Kristin designed the projects and painted the illustrations. Melanie wrote the text and provided creative oversight. Throughout, we have strived to show you that knitting is a simple craft, but one with infinite possibilities. Together, we present a collection of modern heirlooms—garments, accessories, and play things—that we hope you will enjoy knitting and sharing.

Knitting has enriched both our lives. It is through knitting that we became friends and then co-authors. It is through knitting that we have expressed our creativity, found inner calm, and shared joy with our friends and family. We wrote this book in hopes of passing on to you—and your babies—the possibility of such rich and invaluable treasure.

THE BEGINNINGS OF KNITTING ARE
SHROUDED IN MYSTERY. PERHAPS IT
BEGAN IN THE THIRTEENTH CENTURY—
KNITTED SOCKS FROM AROUND THAT
TIME HAVE BEEN FOUND IN EGYPT—
OR PERHAPS IT BEGAN EVEN EARLIER.
WHATEVER THE CASE, IT'S SAFE TO
SAY THAT FOR HUNDREDS OF YEARS
KNITTERS HAVE BEEN TEACHING THEM-
SELVES AND EACH OTHER HOW TO KNIT—
AND THEN KNITTING FOR THEIR BABIES.

GETTING STARTED

DEAN 2 3 4 DR.

chapter 1

While there are those lucky few who knit perfectly from the first stitch (it seems, somehow, that their fingers were born knowing what to do), for most knitters it takes a bit of practice. If you are a member of the former group, congratulations. If you are part of the latter, join the crowd. The first few rows may feel awkward, but we're sure that before too long, probably within a few minutes, you will catch on. Your hands will start to move rhythmically, your eyes will begin to see the logic of the movements, and the knitted fabric will grow. The pace will quicken and the dreams will begin— of blankets and booties, of cardigans and caps, of the love and care and good wishes that you will knit into each and every project, each and every stitch.

5 6 7 8 MADE IN 9 ENGLAND 10 11

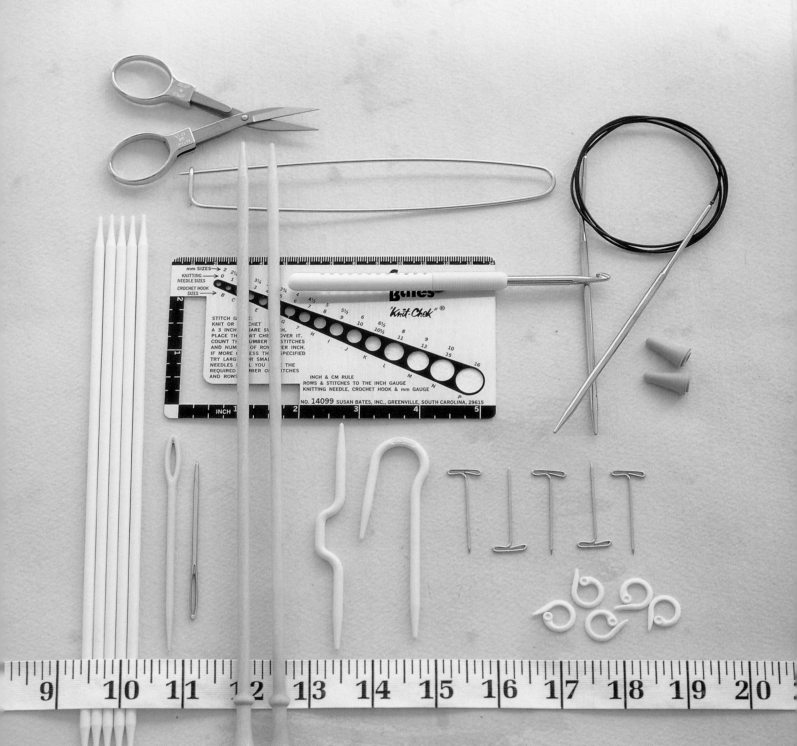

TOOLS OF THE TRADE

The most important tools for knitting are yarn and needles. In fact, with these two basic tools you can get by for a long time. However, there are a few other tools that, while not absolutely necessary, are quite useful.

There are many types of yarn, made of all sorts of fibers, in different thicknesses, and created using a variety of spinning methods. The natural fibers most commonly spun into knitting yarns are wool, alpaca, mohair, cashmere, angora, silk, cotton, and linen. There are also yarns made from synthetic materials like acrylic. The thickness, usually referred to as the weight of the yarn, can range from quite fine to thick. Though the terminology isn't officially standardized, the most common terms you are likely to run across when exploring knitting yarns are, from finest to bulkiest, laceweight, fingering, sport, DK (short for double-knitting), worsted, heavy worsted, chunky, and bulky. For learning to knit, we recommend wool yarn in a worsted, heavy worsted, or chunky weight. Wool is elastic and feels good in the hands and is available in a myriad of beautiful colors. Worsted through chunky weight yarns knit up relatively quickly and offer prompt satisfaction. When choosing yarn with which to learn, more than anything else, we urge you to choose yarn that you love to look at and feel. You will be spending a lot of time with this yarn and your affection for it is likely to influence how much you enjoy knitting. So, please avoid the temptation to start with the cheapest yarn you can find (unless you find a beautiful yarn on sale) or yarn that a friend or relative dug out of her basement for you when she heard you were interested in knitting (unless it happens to be really great).

WINDING A BALL OF YARN

Oftentimes yarn is sold in a skein, which looks like a figure eight. Before you knit with skeined yarn, you have to rewind it into a ball.

To do this, untwist the figure eight and gently open it up into a circle. Place the skein over the back of a chair, over a friend's arms, or around your knees while sitting cross-legged. Sometimes there are yarn or string ties wound through the skein to keep it orderly. Snip any ties, being careful not to cut the main yarn. The two ends of the skein are usually tied together. Find the ends and either cut or untie the knot. Select one end and wind it loosely around your fingers. After a few rounds slip your fingers out and continue winding. Every so often, rotate the ball as you wind to create an even, round shape.

Knitting needles are made in many lengths with many different diameters, ranging from very skinny to very fat, and in a variety of materials, such as aluminum, plastic, wood, and bamboo. They can also be straight with a knob on one end, double-pointed (with points on both ends), or circular (two straight needles connected in the center by a plastic or wire cable). Straight needles and circular needles are used to knit flat pieces of fabric back and forth. Double-pointed and circular needles are used to knit tubular pieces of knitting (instead of knitting back and forth you knit around in a spiral; this is commonly called knitting in the round). American needles come in numbered sizes from 0000 (extremely skinny) to 15 and higher (bordering on broomsticks). In Europe needles are sized using the metric system (which is relevant for American knitters because many European needles are sold in American yarn shops). The thickness of the yarn dictates the needle size required for a project, and the correct sized needle gives the finished knitted fabric a pleasing look, feel, and drape. All knitting patterns list the suggested size and type of needles. All of the projects in this book call for knitting needles in commonly available U.S. sizes.

Although a project that is knit in the round must be knitted on double-pointed or circular needles, beyond that there are few rules in terms of knitting needles. To find the needles that work best and are most comfortable for you, experiment with different types. Consider their weight and texture, how they feel in your hands, and how easily you can maneuver the stitches on them. Keep in mind that you may like one kind of needle for one type of project and another kind for a different project. For example, you may like aluminum needles when working with soft wools and bamboo when working with cashmere. You may like one manufacturer's circular needles and another manufacturer's straight needles. If you break or lose a needle in the middle of a project, try to replace it with a needle made of the same material from the same manufacturer to avoid unevenness and possible changes in gauge at the point of the needle switch.

For convenience, choose a small pair with a blade cover or a pair of folding scissors that can fit into the accessories pouch of a knitting bag.

A tape measure is necessary for taking body measurements and is easy to carry around in a knitting bag. Be aware that tape measures can stretch and become less accurate over time, thus should be replaced accordingly. Rulers and yardsticks, which are easier to position, tend to be more accurate than tape measures when measuring flat pieces of knitting.

NEEDLE GAUGE

Because some needles are not marked with their size, and because some size markings fade over time, it is important to have a needle gauge. Most needle gauges also have inch and/or centimeter markings on them (so they can be used as short rulers) and include handy 2- or 4-inch cutouts to simplify measuring gauge (stitches and rows per inch). Because some needle manufacturers use American sizing terminology and some use the metric system, it is useful to have a needle gauge that includes both systems. To use a needle gauge, slip your needle into the holes, from small to large, until you find the smallest one that fits the needle comfortably.

YARN NEEDLE

(*also known as tapestry needle or darning needle*)
This large, blunt-tipped needle is used to sew pieces of knitting together and to weave loose ends of yarn into the knitted fabric.

CROCHET HOOK

All knitters accidentally drop stitches off their needles from time to time. They can be picked up easily with a crochet hook. The crochet hook should be close to the same size in diameter as the knitting needle being used.

T-PINS OR COIL-LESS SAFETY PINS

It is often useful to pin pieces of knitting in place before sewing them together. T-pins stay in place better than the large plastic pins that are also sold for this purpose. Coil-less, rustproof safety pins work well also. These look like conventional safety pins, except that they have an open, U-shaped bottom, without the familiar doubled coil we are used to seeing. As a result, they are less likely to become caught on your knitting.

CABLE NEEDLE

To create cables, or groups of stitches worked to look like twisted ropes, you exchange groups of stitches using a cable needle. Most knitters choose a cable needle that looks like a large hook or one that looks like a double-pointed needle with a hump in the center. Some knitters skip the cable needle and use a double-pointed knitting needle instead.

STITCH HOLDER

There are times as you knit when you need to set stitches aside to be worked on at a later point. For example, often you will put the neck stitches of a sweater on a holder until you are ready to work the neckband. For these situations, a stitch holder is recommended. You can also create your own stitch holder in a variety of creative ways, by putting stitches to be held on a double-pointed needle and wrapping rubber bands on both ends, or by threading stitches through a shoelace or a piece of scrap yarn.

STITCH MARKERS

Often when you are knitting you are counting stitches and/or rows. To simplify the task, markers can be placed on individual stitches or in between stitches. Closed ring markers can only be placed or removed when you reach the specified stitch on the row. Split ring markers can be placed or removed at any time. Many knitters make their own markers by tying small pieces of yarn in colors that contrast with their work.

POINT PROTECTORS

These small, usually plastic or rubber caps are placed on the points of knitting needles to keep stitches from falling off when you're not working on your knitting project. For a snug fit, be sure to choose point protectors that correspond to the size of your knitting needles.

BASIC KNITTING TECHNIQUES

Often people tell us that they're not good knitters, that all they know how to do is knit and purl. We have news for them: There's not much more to learn. This is the wonder of knitting, what makes it so humble yet so potentially powerful. With two sticks (needles) and a string (yarn) and the knit and purl stitches, you can create a seemingly infinite number of effects. Here we present instructions for casting on (putting stitches on a knitting needle to start), the knit stitch, the purl stitch, and binding off (taking stitches off the needles when you are finished). Learn these techniques and you are on your way to what can easily become a lifelong creative adventure.

CASTING ON

Casting on is the process of putting the first set of stitches on a knitting needle. There are many different ways to do this, each creating a slightly different edge. In this book, we introduce three cast-ons, all of which begin with a slipknot. We suggest that you start with the simple cast-on, which doesn't create as neat an edge as the other two cast-ons, but is, we think, the easiest to learn from a book. That way you can get started quickly. Once you feel comfortable knitting, we suggest that you try the knit-on and long-tail cast-ons, neither of which is hard, just simpler to learn once you are feeling at ease with your yarn and needles.

SLIPKNOT

There are several different ways to make a slipknot, all equally good. So, if you already know how to make a slipknot, there's no need to spend any time looking at these instructions. If you don't know how to make slipknot, here's our favorite method.

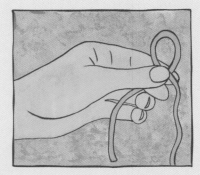

1. About 8 inches from the end of the yarn (called the tail), make a loop with your fingers, passing the working end (the yarn coming from the ball) in front of the tail. With your thumb and forefinger, pinch the space where the two yarns cross each other.

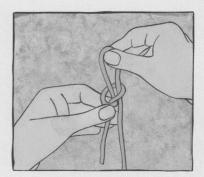

2. Make a second loop with the working yarn right next to the first loop and, from behind, push it, through the first loop about an inch. Pull on the tail to tighten the slipknot.

SIMPLE CAST-ON

Although you are likely to graduate quickly to the more refined cast-ons once you become comfortable knitting, you may continue to use this technique when you desire an especially elastic edge and/or for shaping, that is, to increase one or more stitches at the beginning, end, or in the middle of a row.

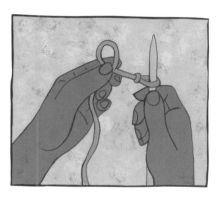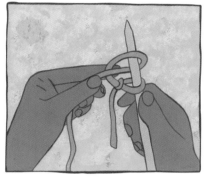

1. Make a slipknot and place it on a knitting needle, pulling it tight enough to stay in one place on the needle but not so tight that it won't move easily if you push it. If your "tail" (the cut end of the yarn) is longer than 5 inches, trim it to 5 inches so that you won't confuse the tail with the working yarn (the yarn coming from the ball). Hold the needle with the slipknot in your right hand and hold the working yarn with the fingers of your left hand. With the fingers of your left hand, shape the working yarn into a loop, with the yarn connected to the slipknot in back.

2. Turn your wrist about 15 degrees so that your knuckles face up and the center of the loop moves over the tip of the needle. Pull the working yarn gently to tighten the stitch on the needle.

   Repeat step 1, from the point when you shape the working yarn into a loop, and step 2 until you have cast on the number of stitches desired. The slipknot is only used once, to create the first stitch on the needle.

CHOOSING A KNITTING BAG

A knitting bag can be anything from a plastic grocery sac to an elaborate lined tote made with antique fabric. Ideally, the fabric should be strong enough to keep knitting needles from poking through, and the bag should include at least one zip-shut pocket for small tools. If you do choose a plastic grocery sac, make sure that it is absolutely clean and has never held raw food, as remnants of the food may attract bugs that can harm your yarn. Picnic baskets (again, untouched by raw food) also work well as knitting "bags."

The long-tail cast-on is one of the most popular. Though it may seem complicated at first glance, it really isn't, so don't lose heart if it takes a little while to get the hang of it. Once you know it, you'll be impressed with its rhythmic quality and how quickly and gracefully your hands can move. Unlike the other two cast-ons in this book, for this one you have to estimate how much yarn you will need before you start. As a general rule, for worsted-weight yarn, allow 1 inch for each stitch to be cast on, then add a few inches as insurance. (For bulkier yarn, allow more; for finer yarn, allow less.)

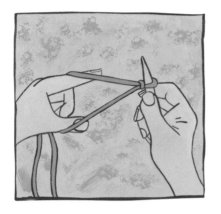 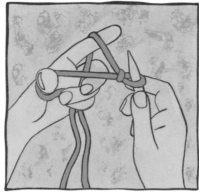 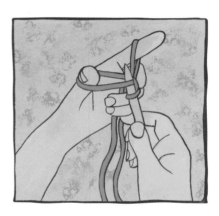

1. Estimate how much yarn you will need based upon the number of stitches you are casting on. For example, if you are casting on 10 stitches in worsted-weight yarn, measure 10 inches plus 2 inches insurance. At the 12-inch mark, make a slipknot on your knitting needle, pulling it tight enough to stay in one place on the needle but not so tight that it won't move easily if you push it. Hold the needle with the slipknot in your right hand. With the fingers of your left hand, grab both the working yarn and the tail about 4 inches or so away from the needle. With your palm facing down,

using your thumb and forefinger, open the space between the working yarn and tail to create a diamond shape with the yarn (the tail will be over your thumb).

2. Flip your wrist so your palm faces up and take a look at your fingers and yarn. Now envision a baseball diamond. The space between the yarn on your forefinger and the needle is first base; the space between the yarn on your thumb and the needle is third base; the space between your forefinger and thumb is the pitcher's mound; and the slipknot on the knitting needle is home plate.

3. Take your knitting needle to third base by sliding it under the space between the yarn on your thumb and up into the center, working from the outside of your thumb (foul territory) inward.

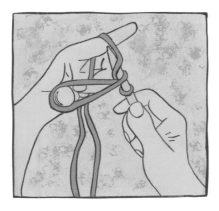

4. Now take the point of the needle to first base by inserting it down into the space formed by the yarn on your forefinger and the needle.

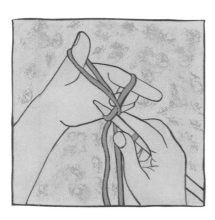

5. Rotate your thumb up and over the needle tip. Remove your thumb from the loop; replace your thumb between the strands as in step 1, and pull on the tail to tighten the new stitch on the needle.

Repeat until you have cast on the number of stitches desired.

KNIT-ON CAST-ON

We suggest that you learn the knit-on cast-on after you have mastered the knit stitch. At that point, learning the knit-on cast-on will be a breeze, taking a couple of minutes or even less.

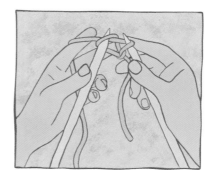

1. Make a slipknot, pulling it tight enough to stay in one place on the needle but not so tight that it won't move easily if you push it. Follow steps 2 through 4 of the knit-stitch instructions on page 16.

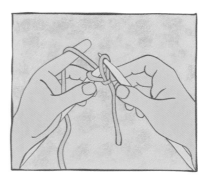

2. Instead of continuing to step 5, insert the left-hand needle from the front down into the center of the stitch on your right-hand needle. Remove the right-hand needle and pull on the working yarn with the fingers of your right hand to tighten the new stitch on your left-hand needle. Return to step 2 of the knit stitch and repeat the casting-on process until you have the desired number of stitches on your needle.

Before beginning to knit, take a moment to examine your cast-on stitches. Note that each stitch looks like a loop with one leg of the loop in front of the needle and one leg of the loop in back of the needle. The stitches on the needle are called live stitches. The cast-on edge runs perpendicular to the live stitches. To complete your first row of knitting you are going to knit into the live stitches. To practice the knit stitch, cast on about 10 stitches and knit row after row until you feel comfortable. Knitting all stitches in this way is called garter stitch. When you feel ready, choose a project from Chapter 2, all of which are made with garter stitch. Note that the style of knitting shown here—our favorite—is called Continental. There are other styles and if a knitter comes along and wants to teach you one of them, welcome the opportunity to expand your skills.

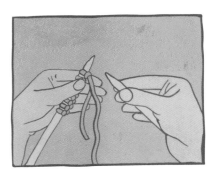

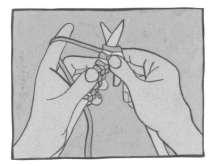

1. With your left hand, pick up your knitting needle with the cast-on stitches. Pick up the other needle with your right hand. Maneuver the stitches on the left-hand needle so that the cast-on edge is in between the two needles. If your "tail" (the yarn with the cut end) is longer than 5 inches, trim it to 5 inches so that you won't confuse the tail with the working yarn (the yarn coming from the ball).

2. Insert the tip of the right-hand needle into the first stitch on the left-hand needle by inserting it under the leg of the loop facing you and up into the center so the needles form an X shape and the needle in your right hand is behind the needle in your left hand. With the thumb and forefinger of your right hand, pinch the two needles together where the two lines of the X intersect.

Pull your working yarn behind and to the left of your left-hand needle and place it between your forefinger and your middle finger with your palm facing away from you. Turn your palm toward your knitting needles and loosely grip your left-hand needle between your thumb (on front of the needle) and your middle finger, ring finger, and pinky (on back of the needle). When your fingers are in the correct position, your forefinger controls the tension on the working yarn. Ideally, the tension on the yarn should be tight enough to keep the yarn in place but not so tight that your fingers hurt.

To help you to remember each step of the knit stitch, try reciting this phrase as you work: "Needle in, yarn around, needle out, stitch off."

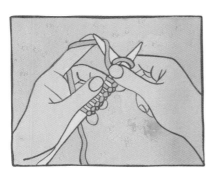

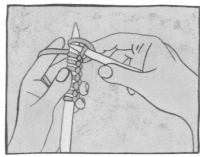

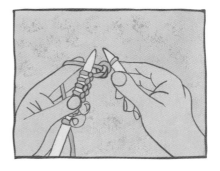

3. Keeping the tension on the working yarn comfortably taut, move the forefinger of your left hand to wrap the working yarn up and over the right-hand needle so that the working yarn ends up in the back of the right-hand needle.

4. Hold the working yarn in place up against the right-hand needle by lightly pressing on it with your right forefinger, and, at the same time, slide the right-hand needle toward you so that you can slide the tip down and out of the center of the stitch on the left-hand needle, bringing the newly-wrapped stitch along with it.

5. Lift the first stitch on the left-hand needle off the needle and let it drop in the space between the two needles. The yarn you wrapped in step 3 has become a new live stitch on your right-hand needle.

Repeat steps 2 through 5 until all of the live stitches on the left-hand needle have been worked and you have a new set of live stitches on your right-hand needle.

To knit the next row and all subsequent rows, switch the needle with the new stitches to your left hand and repeat from step 1.

Once you are comfortable with the knit stitch, the purl stitch, which is the reverse of the knit stitch, is quick and easy to learn. To practice the purl stitch, cast on about 10 stitches and purl every row until you feel comfortable. Next, turn to Chapter 3 and begin exploring the myriad ways the knit stitch and purl stitch can be combined to create common and uncommon textural effects. As you work your stitches, pay attention to the way your needles are making the stitches and the way stitches are sitting on the needles. If you understand stitch construction, you will be able to grasp more advanced techniques easily and will also be able to correct many mistakes easily.

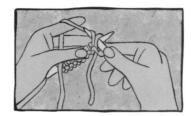

1. Hold the knitting needle with the cast-on stitches in your left hand. Pick up the other needle with your right hand. Maneuver the stitches on the left-hand needle so that the cast-on edge is in between the two needles.

2. Bring the working yarn in front of the left-hand needle by passing it between the two needle tips (don't bring it over the top of a needle because that will create an extra loop on the needles). Insert the tip of the right-hand needle into the first stitch on the left-hand needle by inserting it down into the center of the first stitch and out the front of the stitch. With the thumb and forefinger of your right hand pinch the two needles together where the two needles intersect to steady them. Place the working yarn between your forefinger and your middle finger with your palm facing away from you. Turn your palm toward your knitting needles and loosely grip your left-hand needle between your thumb (on front of the needle) and your middle finger, ring finger, and pinky (on back of the needle). When your fingers are in the correct position, your forefinger controls the tension on the working yarn. Ideally, the tension on the yarn should be tight enough to keep the yarn in place but not so tight that your fingers hurt.

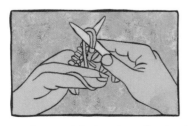

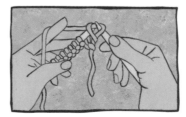

3. Keeping the tension on the working yarn comfortably taut, move your forefinger and your right-hand needle simultaneously and wrap the working yarn around the right-hand needle from front to back so that the yarn ends up close to where it started. Bend the ring finger and forefinger of your left hand at the middle knuckle to hold the working yarn down.

4. Pull the right-hand needle back and out of the stitch on your left needle, bringing the newly wrapped stitch along with it so that the wrapped yarn becomes a new stitch on the right-hand needle. Lift the first stitch off the left-hand needle and let it drop in the space between the two needles. You now have a new live purl stitch on your right-hand needle. Repeat step 2 until all live stitches on the left-hand needle have been worked and you have a new set of live stitches on your right-hand needle. To purl the next row and all subsequent rows, return to step 1.

As you now know, the stitches directly on the knitting needle are called "live" stitches. They are called live because they are in the process of being worked—and, as such, they are the most vulnerable. If you were to remove your knitting needle from a row of live stitches and pull on the working yarn, they would unravel quickly followed by the rows that preceded them. In order to finish off a piece of knitting without risking unraveling, the stitches must be bound off.

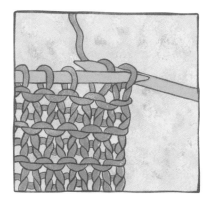

1. At the beginning of your final row, knit 2 stitches as usual. Insert the tip of the left-hand needle into the center of the first stitch knit (the one farthest from the point) on the right-hand needle.

2. Holding the first stitch (the one closest to the point) in place with your right forefinger, lift the second stitch over the tip of the right-hand needle, then remove the left-hand needle so that there is only one stitch remaining on the right-hand needle (the second stitch has "leap-frogged" over the first).

   Knit the next stitch on your left-hand needle so that there are 2 stitches on the right-hand needle again. Leap-frog the second stitch over the first stitch as before. Repeat until all of the stitches on the left-hand needle have been used up and there is only 1 stitch on your right-hand needle.

3. Cut the working yarn about 5 inches or more from the stitch on the needle. Pull on the needle so that the remaining stitch opens up a little. Insert the tip of the cut yarn into the enlarged stitch, remove the needle, and pull on the end of the yarn to tighten.

PICKING UP DROPPED STITCHES

When you knit all stitches in every row, the stitch pattern is called garter stitch. When you alternate knit and purl rows, it is called stockinette stitch. Inevitably, all knitters drop stitches off their needles accidentally, more often, of course, when they are beginners. When a stitch is dropped, it looks like a loose loop, often with one or more horizontal bars that look like ladder rungs above it. The illustrations here show how to pick up dropped stitches in garter stitch and stockinette stitch. While this is easy to do once you are knitting consistently, it can prove to be confusing when you are just beginning and are not absolutely confident about how to form the stitches correctly and how they should sit on the needle. We suggest three options when you are still in the heart of the learning stage: Put aside any perfectionist tendencies and ignore dropped stitches until you have at least mastered the knit stitch; if you can't ignore them, try to remedy the dropped stitches but don't get frustrated if you become confused and drop even more stitches in the process; find a more experienced knitter to pick up the dropped stitches for you (however, only rely on the more experienced knitter briefly, while you are mastering the knit and purl stitches; it is ultimately very important that you are able to pick up your own dropped stitches). Once you feel comfortable and confident with the knit stitch, we recommend that you intentionally drop a few stitches (a horrifying concept to most beginners but definitely a worthwhile exercise in the long run) and practice picking them up, as shown here.

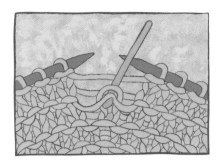

GARTER STITCH

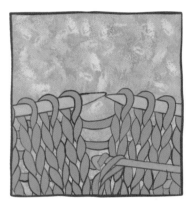

STOCKINETTE STITCH

GARTER STITCH

To fix a dropped stitch in garter stitch, knit to the point in the row where the gap for the dropped stitch is located. Look at your work and determine whether you'll be picking up the stitch and re-creating a row that forms a horizontal ridge or a row that recedes back from the ridges. If you'll be re-establishing a row that forms a ridge (as shown in the illustration at the top of the

page), with the horizontal bar in front of the stitch, insert a crochet hook into the loose stitch from the back, hook the loose bar, and pull it through the stitch from front to back. If that is your only dropped stitch, place it on the left-hand needle so that the right-hand side of the stitch is in front of the needle and the left-hand side of the stitch is in the back of the needle, as shown in the Stitch Mount illustration on page 21.

If your stitch has dropped down several rows, turn the work around and repeat the same process on the other side, being careful to work each horizontal bar in the correct order. Continue in this manner, turning the work after each row until you have worked your way up the ladder of horizontal bars and the dropped stitch has been placed on the left-hand needle.

STOCKINETTE STITCH

To pick up a dropped stitch in stockinette stitch, on the knit (smooth) side of the work, work to the point in the row where the dropped stitch is located. Insert a crochet hook into the dropped stitch from front to back, with the horizontal bar behind the stitch. Hook the horizontal bar, and pull it through the dropped stitch from back to front as shown in the illustration at left. Repeat until all of the horizontal bars have been picked up, being careful to work each of them in the correct order, then place the stitch onto the left-hand needle so that the right-hand side of the stitch is in front of the needle and the left-hand side of the stitch is in back of the needle, as shown in the Stitch Mount illustration at right.

If you are working on a purl-side (bumpy) row and want to pick up dropped stitch(es), work to the point in the row where the dropped stitch(es) occurred, turn the work around so the knit (smooth) side is facing you, and pick up the dropped stitch(es) from the front side of the work as shown here, then return to the purl side and continue.

STITCH MOUNT: STUDYING YOUR STITCHES

Interestingly, people knit differently in different parts of the world. As a result, the way stitches are mounted on the needles varies.

In this book, we teach you Western knitting. As such, when you are looking at a stitch on the needle, its right-hand side should be in front of the needle and its left-hand side should be in the back of the needle. If you are having trouble determining the right-hand and left-hand sides of the stitch, very carefully remove the first stitch on your left-hand needle—it will naturally show you which side is which—then very carefully put the stitch back on the needle. Now compare the stitches on your needle with the illustrations here. The "twisted" stitch is turned on the needle; there are times when stitches are intentionally twisted for decorative purposes, but in standard, everyday Western garter-stitch and stockinette-stitch knitting, they should not be twisted.

STOCKINETTE STITCH

CORRECTLY
MOUNTED
STITCH

TWISTED
STITCH

GARTER STITCH

CORRECTLY
MOUNTED
STITCH

TWISTED
STITCH

FINISHING: WEAVING IN LOOSE ENDS, SEWING SEAMS, AND BLOCKING

The way you sew your seams can, ultimately, determine your level of satisfaction with a project. Like the icing on a cake or the bow on a gift box, beautifully executed seams are the finishing touch that can elevate a project from plain nice to extra-special. While seaming well comes naturally for some people, for most of us it is a learned skill and takes some practice. When you are learning to seam, make sure you have enough time to pay close attention to what you are doing, enough space to work comfortably, and are in a patient state of mind. If you decide that you don't enjoy the seaming process, consider doing more projects that are knitted in the round (these projects generally have very few seams) or talk to the proprietor at your local yarn shop about finishing services that the shop might offer. In most cases, it is advisable to seam a project with the same yarn used to knit it. Exceptions include projects that are knit in yarns that break easily, or lumpy, bumpy novelty yarns, and projects for which you have run out of knitting yarn. Ideally, the substitute seaming yarn should be made of the same kind of fiber as the knitting yarn. If you are knitting with wool and need a seaming yarn, consider using wool tapestry yarn, which is mainly sold for needlepoint. If you are knitting with cotton and need a seaming yarn, try cotton embroidery floss. Tapestry wool and cotton embroidery floss both come in many colors. Always match the color of your seaming yarn and your knitting yarn as closely as possible.

WEAVING IN LOOSE ENDS

When you finish knitting a project, you inevitably have some loose strands of yarn, such as at the cast-on and bind-off edges and in places where you started new balls of yarn.

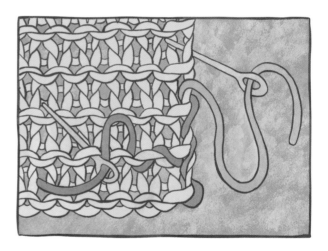

Hiding loose ends by weaving them into the knitted fabric is quick and easy. Simply thread the loose yarn onto a yarn needle and run it over and under the adjacent stitches for about 2 inches, leaving a short (approximately 1-inch tail) on the wrong side of the work. Ideally, the yarn should be woven into the edge of the knitting after seaming, although sometimes weaving into the middle of a piece is unavoidable. After washing or blocking the project with moisture, trim the 1-inch tails to about 1/4 inch.

SEWING SEAMS

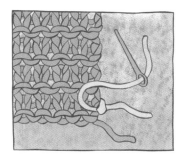

STARTING AND ENDING SEAMS

To start a seam, using a yarn needle, take 2 to 3 small stitches in the same place in the work to anchor the seaming yarn. When you finish sewing a seam, weave the end of the seaming yarn back into the seam just sewn. When estimating how much seaming yarn is needed, allow $1^1/_2$ times the length of the seam, plus several more inches so the yarn can double back on itself securely when threaded on the needle. On large projects, use shorter lengths if long lengths become unwieldly.

MATTRESS STITCH

Mattress stitch, which is nearly invisible, is the most common way to sew pieces of knitting together. The way it is worked varies depending on the struture of the knitted pieces. Shown here are three variations on garter-stitch pieces: Rows to Bind Off, Bind Off to Bind Off, and Rows to Rows. Study the illustrations to learn where the needle enters and exits the stitches on each side of the seam. Mattress stitch is generally worked with the two pieces of knitting butted up against eachother at the edge to be joined, right sides facing up.

ROWS TO BIND OFF

BIND OFF TO BIND OFF

ROWS TO ROWS

OVERCAST STITCH

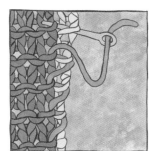

Overcast stitch is easier to master than mattress stitch and is quicker to execute. It can be used when the seaming stitches do not need to be invisible, such as when you are seaming pieces that are highly textured and, thus, the seam stitches will be hidden by the fabric's texture. It can also be used when a project is going to be felted, in which case the seaming stitches will be "absorbed" into the rest of the fabric and will become invisible. Overcast stitch is generally worked with the right sides of the work facing each other.

BLOCKING

When you knit, just about every bit of yarn passes through your fingers. From a sentimental point of view, this imbues the knitting with your love and care. From a practical point of view, this exposes the yarn to some grime and wear and tear. In order to clean the finished product, even out the stitches, and allow the knitting to achieve the correct drape and proportions, it is important to block the pieces of a project either before or after sewing them together. It is also important to block swatches made to check gauge (see right) before starting a project. Blocking involves applying moisture to a project, pinning it out to the desired dimensions (or laying a swatch down to lie flat), and letting it dry. There are numerous blocking methods (and many opinions on which is best). For the projects in this book, we recommend the following techniques.

SWATCHES

To block a swatch, immerse it in a tub of cool water to which you may want to add a small amount of sweater shampoo if the yarn has become soiled while being knitted. (We like to use Wool Wash or Eucalan [available at yarn shops], neither of which requires rinsing; a mild dish detergent; or hair shampoo.) Press on the knitting very lightly to submerge it and saturate the fibers. Allow the swatch to sit in the water for a few minutes. Remove most or all of the water from the tub and gently press on the knitting to release the water. If you have used a sweater shampoo that requires rinsing, remove the swatch from the water, refill the tub with fresh, cool water, resubmerge the swatch, and press on it again. Repeat until all of the shampoo and most of the water has been released.

Place the swatch on a clean towel and roll the towel up sausage-style to release more water. Place the swatch on a dry, flat surface away from direct heat or sunlight to dry, then pin in place without pushing or pulling on the stitches in any way that might distort them. When the swatch is dry, remove the pins and measure the gauge as explained at right.

FINISHED PROJECTS

To block a finished project, follow the instructions for blocking a swatch, removing excess water by either putting the project through the spin cycle in the washing machine or by rolling in a series of clean, dry towels, as follows:

To remove excess water using the washing machine, place the project in a clean pillowcase and close it securely with a knot or with another piece of fabric. Place it in the washing machine and run the spin cycle, being very careful not to accidentally run any of the other cycles. When the spin cycle finishes, carefully remove the damp project from the washer and lay it on a clean, dry towel on a flat surface away from direct heat or sunlight.

To remove excess water using a series of clean, dry towels, carefully remove the project from the tub and transfer it to a clean towel spread on a flat surface that will not be harmed by moisture. With the knitting inside, roll the towel into a sausage shape and press on it to release more water. When the towel you are using is saturated, transfer the knitting to another towel and repeat the "sausage-rolling" process. Continue until the knitting is no longer dripping at all. Lay the damp knitting on a clean, dry towel away from direct heat or sunlight.

Finally, carefully coax the project to the dimensions given in the pattern and, using rust-proof T-pins, pin it in place. Leave undisturbed until completely dry, then remove the pins.

UNDERSTANDING GAUGE

Gauge is one of the most important concepts to understand—and apply—when you are knitting. Gauge is the number of stitches and rows per inch in a piece of knitting. It is determined by the thickness of the yarn, the size of the needles, and the looseness or tightness with which you knit. Every pattern lists the gauge at which it is meant to be knit. For example, all of the projects in Chapter 2 are knit at the gauge of 16 stitches and 32 rows = 4 inches in garter stitch (in other words, 4 stitches and 8 rows per inch when you are knitting every stitch in every row).

If you knit these projects at a different gauge, the finished dimensions will not be what we intended and the fabric will look different. For example, if you knit at a looser gauge (fewer stitches and rows per inch), the dimensions of each project will be larger and the fabric will be less firm. Although needle sizes are always listed in knitting patterns, they are offered in order to give you a place to start. Because every knitter works a little differently, each knitter must check his or her own gauge. Ordinarily, that means casting on enough stitches to make approximately 5 inches worth of knitted width, knitting until the piece is 5 inches high, binding off, then blocking the swatch (see left) as you will the finished project. Once the swatch is dry, you place it on a flat surface, place a ruler on it, and measure the number of rows and stitches in the center 4 inches. If your gauge matches the gauge in

the pattern, you start knitting the project. If it doesn't, you go up or down one or more needle sizes and make another swatch. If you are getting more stitches per inch than stated in the pattern, your stitches are too tight and you need to try bigger needles; if you are getting fewer stitches per inch, your stitches are too loose and you need to try smaller needles. Gauge is measured over 4 inches of a swatch because it is more accurate than trying to measure over just 1 inch. The swatch is knitted larger than 4 inches square for accuracy as well, since it is difficult to measure the edges of a swatch.

While everything we've written so far about gauge is absolutely true, and we would be remiss if we did not encourage you to always knit a gauge swatch, we are going to give you a little break for the projects in Chapter 2. Since the blankets and pillows don't have to fit anyone, and because there is

some leeway with the hat sizing, we suggest that you dive in and begin knitting without the swatch, then measure your gauge when you've competed about 5 inches. If you are pretty close to the gauge in the pattern and you like the way your fabric looks and feels, continue on. If you are way off, start over with a different size needle.

To show you how to count stitches and rows in garter stitch, the rows and stitches are numbered in the illustration above. Garter stitch has some unique stitch properties that make it easy to measure. Unlike other stitch patterns, garter stitch compresses vertically so that two rows measure about the same in height as one stitch in width. It also takes two rows of knitting to create one wavy garter stitch ridge, so when you want to count the number of rows you have worked you can count the ridges and multiply the result by 2.

THE PROJECTS IN THIS CHAPTER ARE ALL MADE WITH GARTER STITCH
SQUARES. BY MAKING THE SQUARES IN DIFFERENT SIZES AND ASSEMBLING
THEM IN VARYING WAYS, YOU CAN MAKE A HAT, A BLANKET, OR A PILLOW.

GARTER STITCH

chapter 2

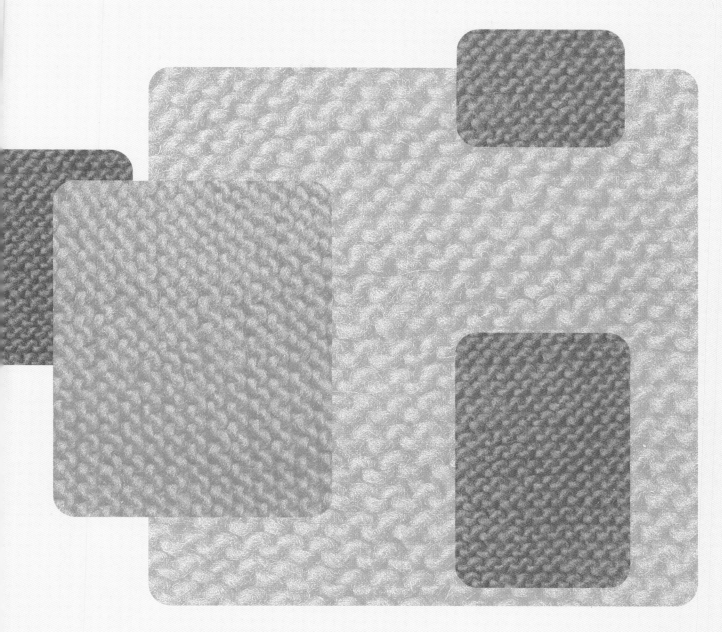

All of these projects are fairly forgiving—if the squares are not quite symmetrical or a few stitches are misshapen, they will still look good. The baby will not know—or care—if they are not "perfect." And the love for the baby that you knit into them will be equally strong regardless.

GARTER STITCH HAT

This hat is made by knitting a rectangle, folding it in half, and sewing the open top and side seam closed. To finish with a hat that is the same size as the one shown in the photo you need to knit it at the gauge listed in the pattern (see page 25 for more about gauge). If you end up with a hat that is a different size, don't worry. It will probably fit the baby at some point; if not, it will surely fit someone else. Once you gain a bit of experience (this could take a few minutes, hours, or days, depending on how quickly you pick up the knit stitch and how much you practice), you will find it very easy to make hats like this in any size you choose. As you begin you may feel like the knitting is controlling you, but soon you will realize that you are controlling your knitting.

FINISHED SIZE

14-inch circumference, one size fits up to 24 months

MATERIALS

1 skein Brown Sheep Lamb's Pride Worsted (4 ounces/190 yards; 85% wool, 15% mohair) in silver #M130 or RPM pink #M105, for body of hat

Small amount of Brown Sheep Lamb's Pride Worsted in brite blue #M57 or silver #130, for pom-pom

1 pair size 9 knitting needles (approximately 10-inch long needles recommended for beginners)

Yarn needle

About 8 T-pins or coil-less safety pins (optional)

4 x 2 1/4-inch piece of cardboard or Pom-Pom Maker tool, for making a pom-pom

Strong scrap yarn (such as a plied wool or cotton yarn), in the same color as the pom-pom

GAUGE

16 stitches and 32 rows = 4 inches on size 9 needles in garter stitch

With silver or pink yarn, loosely cast on 56 stitches. Work in garter stitch (knit all stitches) until piece measures 8 1/2 inches tall; this will take about 68 rows. Bind off loosely.

Place your knitting on a flat surface with the cast-on edge at the bottom and the bind-off edge at the top and measure it. It should be about 14 inches wide and 8 1/2 inches tall. Fold in half so that it measures about 7 inches wide and 8 1/2 inches tall. If desired, hold the edges together with T-pins or safety pins. Using the mattress stitch (see instructions on page 23) and a yarn needle, sew the open side and the top of the hat together. For the side of the hat, follow the illustration marked Rows to Rows. For the top of the hat,

follow the illustration for the seam labeled Bind Off to Bind Off. Using the yarn needle, weave in loose ends of yarn following the illustration on page 22. Stitch the top two corners of the hat together so that they meet in the center. Block the hat as explained on page 24.

Make one pom-pom as explained on page 37. Use the scrap yarn to tie the pieces of the pom-pom together, leaving a tail several inches long when you make the knot. Use the tail to tie the pom-pom to the center of the top of the hat (where the two corners are stitched together). Secure the tail on the inside of the hat.

Fold up the bottom 2 inches or so of the hat to create a cuffed brim.

PATCHWORK & HARLEQUIN BLANKETS

MATERIALS

Brown Sheep Lamb's Pride Worsted
(4 ounces/190 yards;
85% wool, 15% mohair)

FOR PATCHWORK BLANKET
(40 INCHES LONG X 30 INCHES WIDE)
4 skeins oatmeal #M-115
3 skeins Burt's blush #M-189
2 skeins antique mauve #M-85

FOR HARLEQUIN BLANKET
(35 INCHES LONG X 28 INCHES WIDE)
4 skeins blue magic #M-77
3 skeins misty blue #M-76
4 skeins Aran #M-140

FOR BOTH BLANKETS
1 pair size 9 knitting needles,
at least 10 inches long

Yarn needle

GAUGE

16 stitches and 32 rows = 4 inches
on size 9 needles in garter stitch

Both of these blankets are made by knitting and assembling garter-stitch squares. For the Patchwork Blanket at left, large squares are sewn together in straight rows. For the Harlequin Blanket on page 32, smaller squares are turned to look like diamonds, then sewn together for a blanket with a zigzag edge. If you are a beginner, your squares/diamonds may not all be exactly the same size. With a little fudging when you're sewing the pieces together, you should still finish with a beautiful blanket. In addition, blocking (see page 24) can even out some of the size differences. Patchwork and Harlequin Blankets are wonderful group projects, with friends and family of the new baby each providing a square and one person sewing them all together. To give a baby shower a new twist, enlist a friend or hire a teacher (or be the teacher yourself, if you're ready) to show the guests how to knit squares, and then sew the squares together to make a blanket to present to the baby and the adoring parents. Although some of the squares may turn out more "primitive-looking" than others, after blocking and sewing, the blanket will become a beautiful testament to the spirit of the shower and the love and good wishes of the makers—a true heirloom.

PATCHWORK BLANKET

To make this blanket as shown in the photo at left you will need to make 12 garter-stitch squares in the following colors: 6 oatmeal, 4 Burt's blush, and 2 antique mauve. Start as many squares as possible with enough yarn to complete the entire square. Each skein of yarn will make about 1 3/4 squares. If you run out of yarn mid-square, start a new ball as explained on page 33.

To make a square, using size 9 needles, cast on 40 stitches. Work in garter stitch (knit all stitches) for 10 inches. Bind off all stitches. Weave in loose ends of yarn along edges (see page 22). If you are knitting to gauge, each square will measure 10 inches along each side.

Arrange the squares in the color order shown on page 30, or in any way that you like. Using the mattress stitch (see page 23), the oatmeal-colored yarn, and a yarn needle, sew the squares together using the Rows to Bind Off seam so that the garter ridges of each square alternate between running right-to-left and up-and-down. The blanket is sewn together in this way to create stability (to keep it from stretching out). Block the blanket as explained on page 24 to even out the stitches and give it a finished, professional look.

HARLEQUIN BLANKET

To make this blanket as shown in the photo at left you will need to make 32 garter-stitch squares in the following colors: 12 blue magic, 12 Aran, and 8 misty blue. Start as many squares as possibe with enough yarn to complete the entire square. Each skein of yarn will make about 3 3/4 squares. If you run out of yarn mid-square, start a new ball of yarn as explained at right.

To make a square, using size 9 needles, cast on 28 stitches. Work in garter stitch (knit all stitches) for 7 inches. Bind off all stitches. Weave in loose ends of yarn along edges (see page 22). If you are knitting to gauge, each square will measure 7 inches along each side.

Turn the squares so that they are oriented as diamonds and arrange the colors as shown in the photo at left or in any way that you like. Using the mattress stitch (see page 23), the Aran yarn, and a yarn needle, sew the diamonds together using the Rows to Bind Off seam so that the rows of adjacent diamonds alternate the direction of the garter ridges. The blanket is sewn together in this way to create stability (to keep it from stretching out). Block the blanket as explained on page 24 to even out the stitches and give it a finished, professional look.

STARTING A NEW BALL OF YARN

You will need to start a new ball of yarn when you come close to the end of the one you are using or when you want to change colors. Try to plan it so that you are changing to the new yarn at the beginning of a row.

Cut the old yarn, leaving an approximately 4-inch tail. Tie the new yarn to the old yarn with a knot, sliding the knot as close as possible to the last stitch knitted with the old yarn and leaving an approximately 4-inch tail of the new yarn. Start knitting with your new yarn. When you are finished knitting the project, weave the loose ends along the side seams or edges of your work.

FOR LARGE SOLID-COLOR CUSHION
4 skeins khaki #M18
1 skein RPM pink #M105

FOR PATCHWORK CUSHION
1 skein periwinkle #M59
1 skein RPM pink #M105
2 skeins Aran #M140

FOR TWO-COLOR CUSHION
2 skeins RPM pink #M105
2 skeins sapphire #M65
1 skein khaki #M18

FOR ALL CUSHIONS
1 pair size 9 knitting needles (for the
single-color and two-color cushions
they should be long enough to accommodate 48 or 64 stitches), either
14-inch straight or 29-inch circular

Yarn needle

16-inch-square pillow form,
for large solid-color cushion

14-inch-square pillow form,
for patchwork cushion

12-inch square pillow form,
for two-color cushion

4 x 2 1/4-inch piece of cardboard
or Pom-Pom Maker tool,
for making pom-poms

Strong scrap yarn (such as a
plied wool or cotton yarn), in the
same color as the pom-poms

GAUGE

16 stitches and 32 rows = 4 inches
on size 9 needles in garter stitch

BABY CUSHIONS

These cushions transform a hard floor into a soft play area for baby. One at a time, they are also comfortable to use while rocking and feeding. This is a good project for a long car trip or for a commute on a bus or train because, once you have mastered the knit stitch, it doesn't require a lot of concentration; the knitting becomes rhythmic and relaxing—a meditation of sorts.

The cushion is shown in three variations. The single-color version is made by knitting one very large rectangle, then folding it to make a square "envelope" for the pillow insert. The patchwork cushion is made by sewing together eight squares, four for each side. The two-color cushion is a different color on each side. Because the single-color and two-color cushions require knitting a lot of stitches at the same time, we recommend that you use straight needles that are at least 14 inches long or circular needles on which you knit back and forth (see instructions on page 36). Some people find 14-inch needles cumbersome, which is why we are introducing circular needles here.

LARGE SOLID-COLOR CUSHION

With khaki yarn and size 9 needles, cast on 64 stitches. Work in garter stitch (knit all stitches) for 36 inches (approximately 288 rows). Bind off. If you are knitting to gauge you will have a rectangular that measures 16 inches wide and 36 inches high. Weave in loose ends of yarn as shown on page 22. Block according to the instructions on page 24 to even out the stitches and to give the cushion cover a finished, profes- sional look.

On a long, flat surface, position the knitted rectangle lengthwise so that the garter ridges are traveling up and down (not across the piece). Fold the cast-on edge and the bind- off edges in toward the center and overlap them by 2 inches. Using mattress stitch (see page 23), a yarn needle, and the khaki yarn, sew together the top and bottom seams, sewing together all three layers at the points where the edges overlap. You now have a large envelope with an opening in the center of one side to insert the pillow form.

KNITTING BACK & FORTH ON CIRCULAR NEEDLES

When you are working on a project with a lot of stitches, it is often more comfortable and easier to knit back and forth on long, circular needles than on long, straight needles. This is because circular needles are made in longer sizes than straight needles (so they can hold more stitches without cramming).

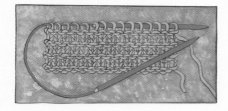

To work back and forth on circular needles, pretend that you are working on two straight needles that happen to be joined at their ends, and cast on and knit as usual, as shown in the illustration.

Using the pink yarn, make 3 pom-poms (see instructions at right) and attach them, in a line, evenly spaced, along the edge of the envelope opening. Alternatively, attach the pom-poms in any way that you like.

PATCHWORK CUSHION

Make 8 squares (2 periwinkle, 2 RPM pink, and 4 Aran) as follows: With size 9 needles, cast on 28 stitches. Work in garter stitch (knit all stitches) for 7 inches (approximately 56 rows). If you are knitting to gauge, the squares will measure 7 inches along each side. Bind off all stitches. Weave in loose ends of yarn as shown on page 22. On a flat surface, arrange the squares as shown in the photograph on page 34 or as desired. Using the mattress stitch illustration on page 23, a yarn needle, and the Aran yarn, sew four squares together using the Rows to Bind Off seam so that the garter ridges alternate between running right-to-left and up-and-down. Repeat with the remaining four squares. You now have two larger squares, each made up of four smaller squares, measuring about 14 inches on each side. Block according to the instructions on page 24 to even out the stitches and to give the cushion cover a finished, professional look. When dry, sew the two patchwork

squares together on three sides. Insert pillow form and sew the fourth side closed.

TWO-COLOR CUSHION

With pink yarn and size 9 needles, cast on 48 stitches. Work in garter stitch (knit all stitches) for 12 inches (approximately 96 rows). Bind off all stitches. If you are knitting to gauge you will have a square that measures 12 inches on each side. Make a second square with sapphire yarn. Weave in loose ends of yarn as shown on page 22. Block according to the instructions on page 24 to even out the stitches and to give the cushion cover a finished, professional look. When dry, using the mattress stitch, a yarn needle, and either color of yarn, sew the two squares together on three sides. Make 4 pom-poms with khaki yarn following the instructions at right. Attach the pom-poms to the four corners of the cushion cover. Insert pillow form and sew the fourth side closed.

MAKING POM-POMS

While we were making the pom-poms for the projects in this chapter we rediscovered their visual and tactile appeal. Before attaching them to the hats and pillows, we found ourselves tossing them from hand to hand, squeezing them, and admiring the way they looked and felt. In a visceral kind of way, they seemed to momentarily take us back to childhood. If you don't want to make pom-poms by hand, try the jumbo or regular-size Pom-Pom Maker from Clover. We were skeptical at first (it seemed crazy to spend even a little bit of money on such a thing) but when we tried it we were hooked. We loved churning out full, fluffy pom-poms one after another.

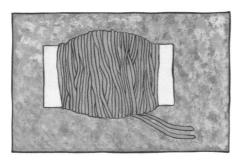

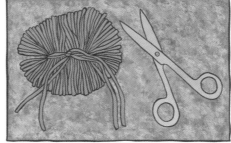

STEP 1

To make an approximately 2-inch diameter pom-pom (the size we recommend for the projects in this chapter), cut a piece of stiff cardboard to measure 4 inches by 2¼ inches. Measure approximately 12 yards of yarn from the ball but don't cut it. Double the yarn on itself (so you have about 6 working yards) and, still without cutting it, wrap the double strands around the short side of the cardboard approximately 70 times, leaving about ½ inch at each end of the cardboard free.

STEP 2

Fold a 24-inch piece of strong, plied yarn in half (if the yarn you're using for the pom-pom is not strong and plied, use scrap yarn in a coordinating color). Carefully slip the wrapped yarn off the cardboard. Using the plied yarn, tie a tight double knot in the center of the wrapped bundle (around the "waistline" of the strands). Turn the bundle over and tie a second double knot on the opposite side, leaving tails to use for securing the pom-pom to the knitting. Cut the loops at each side using a sharp-pointed scissors. Over a wastebasket, fluff out and trim the cut loops to form a neat, evenly shaped ball.

ALL OF THE PROJECTS IN CHAPTER 2 WERE
MADE SOLELY WITH THE KNIT STITCH. ALL OF
THE PROJECTS IN THIS CHAPTER—AND MOST
OF THE REST OF THE BOOK—COMBINE THE KNIT
STITCH AND THE PURL STITCH, INSTRUCTIONS
FOR WHICH APPEAR ON PAGES 16 AND 18,
RESPECTIVELY. IF YOU EITHER KNIT OR PURL
ALL STITCHES IN ALL ROWS, YOU PRODUCE
GARTER STITCH. HOWEVER, IF YOU ALTERNATE
ONE KNIT ROW WITH ONE PURL ROW, YOU WILL
PRODUCE STOCKINETTE STITCH, THE MOST
COMMON STITCH IN KNITTING.

THE PURL STITCH
& A NEW WORLD
OF TEXTURE

chapter 3

Fabric created from stockinette stitch is smooth on the knit side (usually considered the right side) and bumpy on the purl side (usually considered the wrong side). In addition to alternating knit rows with purl rows, you can also mix these two stitches within a single row. For example, if you alternate knit and purl stitches across a row with an even number of stitches (knit 1, purl 1, knit 1, purl 1, etc.) you will create ribbing, which is most commonly used for the bottom edges of sweater bodies and sleeves and for neckbands. Six different knit-purl combinations are showcased in the Stitch-Sampler Baby Blocks on page 40.

STITCH-SAMPLER BABY BLOCKS

MATERIALS

1 ball Dale of Norway Freestyle (50 grams/88 yards; 100% machine-washable wool) in each of the following six colors: hot pink #4417, lupine blue #5533, turquoise #6135, orange/gold #3227, light green #9133, and electric blue #5444

One pair size 9 knitting needles, or size needed to obtain gauge, plus one pair of needles two sizes smaller than the main needles for basketweave swatch

T-pins

Yarn needle

1 3-inch foam cube (available from some craft stores or custom-cut from an upholstery store), for each block

GAUGE

4 stitches and 5 rows = 1 inch on larger needles in stockinette stitch

These baby blocks captivate children of all ages. For each one, you make six swatches, each using a different stitch pattern, then you sew the swatches together and stuff with a foam cube. We made six blocks so that we could show all six stitch patterns, each in a different color, in one photograph. If you want to scale down the project, consider making fewer blocks or using the same color for more than one side of each block. Keep in mind that each ball of yarn will make about 15 to 16 swatches, and plan from there. On pages 43 and 44 are illustrations that show you what each swatch will look like. Take some time to study these illustrations and your knitting. It will be of tremendous help as you begin to take on more challenging projects. We used machine-washable wool for this project. Wool yarn is made machine-washable either by coating it with a thin layer of resin or manipulating the surface of the wool chemically so its scales cannot interlock and felt together, which causes shrinking. If wool is not labeled machine-washable (sometimes called superwash) it must be washed by hand.

To make one block, make one each of the six swatches. If you want to make blocks like the ones shown in the photo, make each swatch in a different color. Each finished swatch should measure about 3 1/4" square. Measure the swatches as you work and adjust the number of rows, if necessary, to finish with the correct size. Blocking can even out slight differences in size.

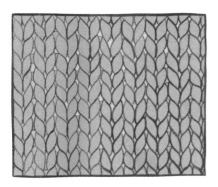 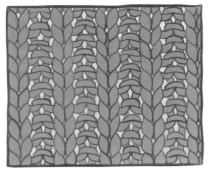 

STOCKINETTE STITCH

This is the most common stitch in knitting. Usually the smooth (knit) side is considered the right side, and the bumpy (purl) side is the wrong side. When this is reversed and the purl stitch is considered the right side, it is called reverse stockinette stitch. Stockinette stitch naturally curls toward its purl face at the sides, and toward its knit face at the top and bottom. The curling is not evident when pieces of stockinette stitch knitting are sewn together. It is controlled when non-curling borders, such as garter stitch, seed stitch, or ribbing, are worked at the edges.

Using size 9 needles, cast on 14 stitches.

ROW 1: Knit
ROW 2: Purl

Repeat rows 1 and 2 until you have completed 17 rows or the swatch measures 3¹/4 inches square. Bind off loosely.

1 X 1 RIBBING

Ribbing is most commonly used to pull in the edges of sweaters, such as at the bottom edges and sleeve cuffs. Because it is elastic, it contracts from side to side.

Using size 9 needles, cast on 14 stitches.

ALL ROWS: Knit 1, purl 1, repeat to end of row, and end with the last stitch as purl 1.

Continue in 1 x 1 ribbing until you have completed 19 rows or the swatch measures 3¹/4 inches square. Bind off loosely.

2 X 2 RIBBING

2 x 2 ribbing is slightly more elastic than 1 x 1 ribbing.

Using size 9 needles, cast on 14 stitches.

ROW 1: Knit 2, purl 2, repeat to end of row, and end with the last 2 stitches as knit 2.

ROW 2: Purl 2, knit 2, repeat to end of row, and end with the last 2 stitches as purl 2.

Continue in 2 x 2 ribbing until you have completed 19 rows or the swatch measures 3¹/4 inches square. Bind off loosely.

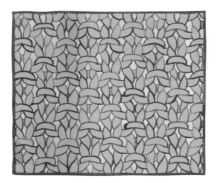 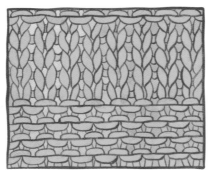 

SEED STITCH

Seed stitch is often used in the body of garments, especially at the side panels in heavily cabled sweaters, and as an edging on sweaters, such as at the bottom border or neck edge. It is easily created by knitting the purl stitches and purling the knit stitches as you proceed from row to row.

Using size 9 needles, cast on 13 stitches

ALL ROWS: Knit 1, purl 1, repeat to end of row, and end with the last stitch as knit 1.

Continue in seed stitch until you have completed 20 rows or the swatch measures 3¹/4 inches square. Bind off loosely.

REVERSE STOCKINETTE RIDGES

By interrupting the knit rows of stockinette stitch with extra purl rows, you create decorative ridges. These ridges, carefully placed to create specific patterns, are commonly used to embellish traditional British fisherman's sweaters known variously as ganseys, guernseys, or jerseys.

Using size 9 needles, cast on 14 stitches.

ROW 1: Purl all stitches.
ROW 2: Knit all stitches.
ROW 3: Purl all stitches.
ROW 4: Knit all stitches.
ROW 5: Knit all stitches.
ROW 6: Purl all stitches.
ROW 7: Knit all stitches.
ROW 8: Purl all stitches.

Repeat Rows 1 through 8 for the number of rows necessary for the swatch to measure 3¹/4 inches square. Bind off loosely.

BASKETWEAVE STITCH

You need more stitches to show the basketweave stitch than required for the stitch patterns in the other swatches. In order to finish with a swatch that is comparable in size to the others, it is, therefore, necessary to knit this swatch with needles two sizes smaller than the others (with smaller needles, the stitches pull together more, thus take up less space and make the square smaller).

Using size 7 needles, cast on 16 stitches.

ROWS 1–4: Knit 4, purl 4, repeat to end of row, and end with the last 4 stitches as purl 4.

ROWS 5–8: Purl 4, knit 4, repeat to end of row, and end with the last 4 stitches as knit 4.

Repeat rows 1 through 8 for the number of rows necessary for the swatch to measure approximately 3¹/4 inches square, ending after having knitted either Row 4 or Row 8 to complete the last strip of basketweave. Bind off loosely.

FINISHING

Block all pieces according to the instructions on page 24 and pin them out to 3 1/4 inches square to dry. Using the mattress stitch and a yarn needle, sew 4 swatches together side by side so you are stitching rows to rows following the illustration at right. If desired, to make your seams as invisible as possible, work the mattress stitch one stitch in from each side (you will lose 1 stitch on each side in the seam). Sew together the left side of the first swatch to the right side of the last swatch to make a closed circle of swatches. Sew the fifth swatch to the top or bottom. Place the foam cube inside and sew the sixth swatch in place to close.

SEWING TOGETHER STOCKINETTE-STITCH PIECES WITH MATTRESS STITCH

In Chapter 1 we introduced mattress stitch as a method for sewing together pieces of garter-stitch knitting. Here we show how to work mattress stitch on stockinette-stitch pieces. This method works equally well on other pattern stitches, such as those featured in the Stitch-Sampler Baby Blocks. With the edges of the two pieces to be sewn together butted up against each other and right sides facing you, insert the needle under two horizontal bars at one edge of the piece, then under the corresponding two horizontal bars on the other piece. Every few rows, pull on the sewing yarn to draw the pieces together and close the seam. Try to match the tension of the knitting, and do not pull so tight that the seam puckers.

BASKETWEAVE TOWEL OR BLANKET

MATERIALS

FOR 38-INCH-SQUARE TOWEL
OR BLANKET

8 skeins Crystal Palace Cotton
Chenille (50 grams /98 yards; 100%
cotton) in pale pink #6752

One size 4 circular needle, 29 inches
or longer, or size needed to obtain
gauge

2 stitch markers

GAUGE

14 stitches and 26 rows = 4 inches
on size 4 needles in basketweave stitch

Knitted in soft, absorbent, machine-washable cotton chenille, this project works equally well as a towel or blanket. To give the project a finished look, the basketweave stitches are framed by garter stitch. Stitch markers are used as a visual cue to show you where the garter stitch edge stops and the basketweave begins (and vice versa). Because this project begins with 136 stitches (and it's not always easy to keep that many stitches on a straight needle) we recommend you use a 29-inch or longer circular needle. See the illustration on page 36 to learn how to knit back and forth on circular needles. In Chapter 5, you will learn how to knit in the round on circular needles.

MAKE A GAUGE SWATCH

Before starting the towel or blanket, make a gauge swatch to make sure you are using the correct size needles and to practice the basketweave stitch while working back and forth on circular needles. When you are done, you can use the swatch as a mini washcloth.

To make the swatch, cast on 24 stitches and work in basketweave stitch as follows:

ROW 1: For the swatch, knit 8 stitches, purl 8 stitches, knit 8 stitches. For the towel/blanket, knit 8 stitches, purl 8 stitches, then repeat to the end of the row, and end with the last 8 stitches as knit 8.

ROW 2: For the swatch, purl 8 stitches, knit 8 stitches, purl 8 stitches. For the towel/blanket, purl 8 stitches, knit 8 stitches, then repeat to the end of the row, and end with the last 8 stitches as purl 8.

Repeat rows 1 and 2 five more times for a total of 12 rows.

ROW 13: For the swatch, purl 8 stitches, knit 8 stitches, purl 8 stitches. For the towel/blanket, purl 8 stitches, knit 8 stitches, then repeat to the end of the row, ending as above with purl 8.

ROW 14: For the swatch, knit 8 stitches, purl 8 stitches, knit 8 stitches. For the towel/blanket, knit 8 stitches, purl 8 stitches, then repeat to the end of the row, ending as above with knit 8.

Repeat rows 13 and 14 five more times for a total of 12 rows; there are now 24 rows total.

ROWS 25-36 (SWATCH ONLY): Repeat rows 1–12 for a total of 36 rows on swatch. Bind off loosely.

Block your swatch as you will the finished towel/blanket (see page 24). Lay your work on a flat surface and count the number of stitches and rows over 4 inches. You are aiming for 14 stitches and 26 rows, but because the towel is not worn and does not need to "fit," you don't have to match this gauge exactly— just try to get close. However, if you are not satisfied with the way your swatch looks, and you have more stitches and rows than the gauge (indicating that your stitches are too tight), go up a needle size or two; if you have fewer stitches and rows than the gauge (indicating that your stitches are too loose), go down a needle size or two.

If you are making the towel/ blanket for a baby, make sure your knitting is tight enough to assure that fingers and toes won't easily get caught in the stitches. Be aware that if you do not knit to gauge, you may need more yarn than specified.

MAKE THE TOWEL/BLANKET

Cast on 136 stitches. Work in garter stitch (knit all stitches) for 2 inches.

ROW 1: Establish block pattern with garter edge as follows: Knit 8 stitches. Place a marker on the right-hand needle directly after the 8 stitches you have just finished knitting. Work row 1 of basketweave stitch (see left) over the center 120 stitches (until there are 8 stitches left), place a marker and knit the last 8 stitches.

ROWS 2 THROUGH 24: Work 8 stitches in garter stitch (knit every row), then transfer the marker from your left-hand to your right-hand needle. Work basketweave stitch as explained at left. When you reach the second marker, transfer it to your right-hand needle and work the remaining 8 stitches in garter stitch. When you have finished 24 rows total (which is one complete pattern repeat), return to row 1 of the basketweave stitch and start over.

Work as established in garter and basketweave stitch until your towel/ blanket measures 36 inches and you have completed row 12 or row 24 of basketweave stitch. (This will give a balanced look to your towel/blanket.) Work 2 inches in garter stitch. Bind off loosely. Weave in loose ends (see page 22). Block according to the instructions on page 24.

STORING HANDKNITS
PLANNING FOR GENERATIONS TO COME

In order to keep handknits looking fresh and wearable for generations, it is important to launder and store them with care. Here are some helpful hints:

Before putting handknits away for a season or until the next child is ready to use and/or wear them, make sure that they are completely clean. Bugs that destroy fibers are especially attracted to food stains and body oils that may rest on clothing. This kind of residue can also, over time, degrade the fiber.

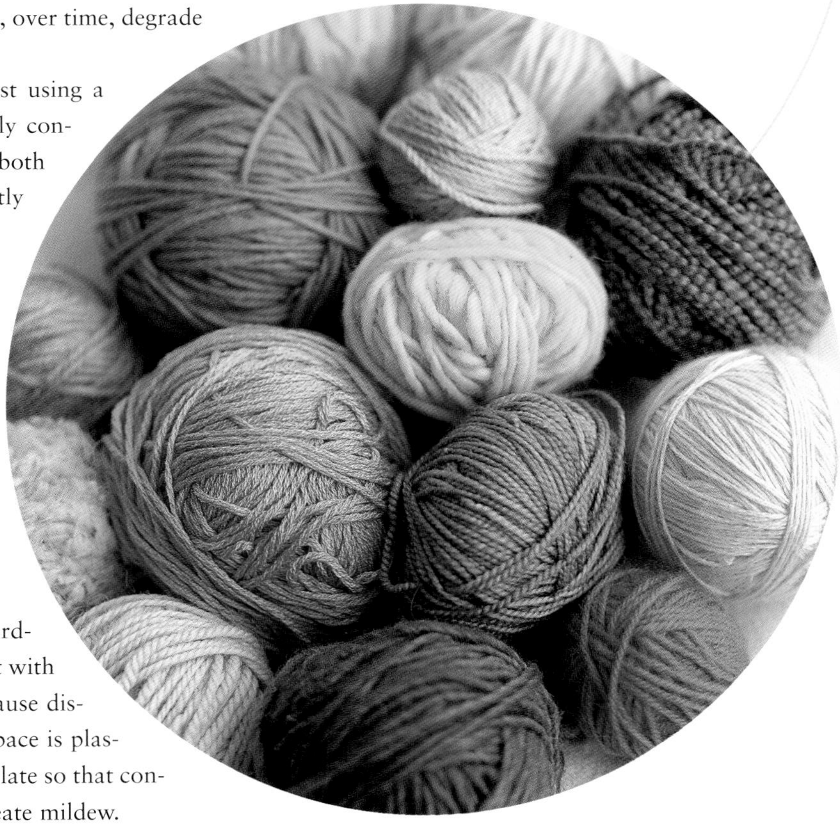

To launder handknits, we suggest using a mild detergent or shampoo. Especially convenient are Eucalan and Wool Mix (both sold in yarn shops), which clean gently and do not need to be rinsed out.

Store handknits, neatly folded, in chests or drawers. In general, we do not recommend hanging handknits because their weight can cause them to stretch. However, because many baby items are small and very lightweight, hanging on padded hangers can be an acceptable option if drawer or chest space is not available.

If the storage space is wood or cardboard, both of which are acidic, line it with acid-free paper; acidic surfaces can cause discoloration over time. If the storage space is plastic, leave enough room for air to circulate so that condensation does not form and then create mildew.

Store handknits with sachets of strong-smelling herbs, such as lavender or cedar. The strong smells will throw fiber-damaging insects off the trail. Replace the herbs in the sachets when the scent begins to fade; revive cedar products by sanding them lightly or rubbing them with cedar oil. Do not allow the cedar or herbs to come in direct contact with the handknits because the oils in them can stain the fiber. Avoid using mothballs as the active ingredient in them, napthalene, is poisonous and can cause ill health.

NOW THAT YOU KNOW THE KNIT AND PURL STITCHES, IT IS TIME TO LEARN SHAPING, WHICH IS A SIMPLE MATTER OF INCREASING AND DECREASING STITCHES. ON PAGES 52 AND 53 ARE INSTRUCTIONS FOR THREE INCREASE TECHNIQUES (ADDING A STITCH WHERE THERE WASN'T ONE BEFORE) AND TWO DECREASE TECHNIQUES (REDUCING TWO STITCHES TO ONE STITCH) USED IN THE PROJECTS IN THIS BOOK.

S H A P I N G

chapter 4

In the Baby's First Ball pattern we introduce another technique called short-rowing. When you work short rows, instead of knitting each row from end to end, you work partway across a row, then turn the project around and work back across the same stitches again. In effect, you are knitting more rows on certain stitches than others, thus creating extra fabric in strategic places. It can be compared to adding an extra panel in the belly section of maternity clothes.

TECHNIQUES FOR INCREASING AND DECREASING

These are the most basic increases and decreases, and they could conceivably take you through a lifetime of knitting. There are many other interesting shaping methods to learn if you feel so inclined, and many knitters are excited to expand their repertoires and continuously refine their work using more advanced techniques. Often knitting patterns do not specify which increase or decrease to use, so it is helpful to pay attention to what each one looks like and the effect it has on the fabric. That way, when the time comes, you can choose the increase or decrease that is best suited for your situation.

INCREASES

KNITTING INTO THE FRONT AND BACK OF A STITCH

To increase using this method, knit into the first stitch on your left-hand needle as usual but do not lift the old stitch off the left-hand needle (below left). Instead, knit this stitch a second time by inserting the right-hand needle down into the center of the stitch (below right), wrap the yarn, pull up another new loop from the same stitch, then slip the original stitch off the left-hand needle. There are now two stitches on your right-hand needle instead of the usual one. The one on the right looks like an ordinary knit stitch; the stitch on the left has a horizontal "bump," at its base making it look like a purl stitch. This kind of increase is sometimes abbreviated as "kf&b."

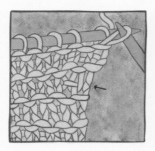 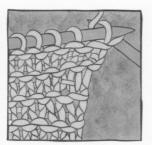

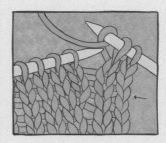

SIMPLE CAST-ON INCREASE

This method of increasing is performed in the exact same manner as the simple cast-on presented in Chapter 1. In that chapter, we present the simple cast-on as a method of putting all the stitches you need for a project on the needle at the same time. When used as an increase, the simple cast-on stitches are added to stitches already on the needle, at the beginning or end of a row, and sometimes even in the middle of a row between live stitches. Some knitting patterns call this a backward loop increase. To make this increase, form a loop with the working end of the yarn and place it on the right-hand needle in the middle of or at the end of a row, or on the left-hand needle at the beginning of a row. Pull gently on the working yarn so each increase loop has the same tension as the live stitches. On the next row, work the increase loops just as you would cast-on stitches.

YARNOVER INCREASE

Yarnover increases are often found in the middle of a piece. To make a yarnover, knit to the point where the yarnover is to be placed. Instead of knitting the next stitch on the left-hand needle, wrap the working yarn from front to back around the right-hand needle. Knit the rest of the stitches on the left-hand needle as usual. On the next row, pay attention to where the yarnover is located and make sure you knit it (it is easy to let it drop off the needle if you're not paying attention). Yarnovers leave small holes in the work, which are desirable in lace knitting. In the illustration at right the yarnovers are used as increases as in the Easy Eyelet Washcloth or Blanket on page 58. They are also sometimes paired with a decrease to make buttonholes. Yarnover is commonly abbreviated as "yo."

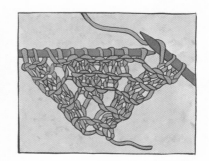

DECREASES

KNIT 2 TOGETHER

To decrease 1 stitch by knitting 2 stitches together, insert your right-hand needle into the first 2 stitches of your left-hand needle, and knit them both together in the same way you would knit 1 stitch, making sure you drop both stitches from the left-hand needle when you finish. This type of decrease slants slightly to the right. It is abbreviated as "k2tog." Two stitches can be purled together in the same manner.

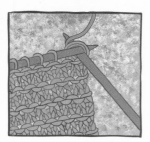

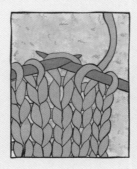 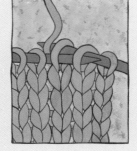

SLIP SLIP KNIT

This decrease can be divided into two parts:

PART 1 (slip 2 stitches, one at a time, knitwise; above left): Insert right-hand needle into next stitch on left-hand needle as if you are going to knit it, but instead of knitting it, simply slip it onto the right-hand needle. Slip the next stitch in the same way.

PART 2 (knit 2 stitches together; above right): To complete the decrease, insert left-hand needle into the front loops of both slipped stitches, wrap yarn around right-hand needle, and knit the 2 stitches together as if they were one stitch. This decrease slants to the left. It is abbreviated "ssk."

BABY'S FIRST BALL

MATERIALS

1 skein JCA Turnberry
Tweed (100 grams/220
yards; 100% wool) in two or
more of the following colors,
depending on how many
balls you want to make and
how many colors you want
to use for each ball: gold
#30, magenta #66, cobalt
blue #32, purple #33,
turquoise #36, and olive #67

1 pair size 7 knitting needles

Yarn needle

4 large handfuls of clean,
raw wool, or wool yarn
scraps, or 2 large handfuls
of polyester fiberfill per ball,
for stuffing

GAUGE

Gauge is not important in
this project since the ball
will be felted. If you use a
different yarn than called
for in this pattern, follow
the needle size recommended
on the label for that yarn.

The idea for these knitted balls came from a 19th-century knitting book. When you make them, you are following in the footsteps of many a knitter. And when babies play with them, they are carrying on a longstanding tradition. After the outside of these balls is knitted, they are felted by running them through the washing machine. The agitation of the machine causes the wool fibers to shrink and adhere to each other to produce a dense, impermeable fabric. We stuffed our balls with raw wool fiber (that is, wool that has been removed from the sheep and cleaned, but not yet spun into yarn). Other options are polyester fiberfill (which creates a particularly lightweight and spongy ball) or wool yarn scraps. We also like to put small cat bell toys or rattles in our balls as long as there is no chance of the balls being torn open. If that happens, the loose bell could become a choking hazard. Amazingly, these balls are knitted back and forth in garter stitch on straight knitting needles. The ball shape is created by employing a very simple technique called short-rowing, which is explained in the pattern.

MAKE THE BALL SHAPE

For a one-color ball, follow the instructions using the same color throughout. To make a two-color ball, choose two colors and call one Color A and the other Color B. To make a multicolored ball, change colors as desired at the beginning of each new section. To help to keep track of your place in the pattern, take note of where your cast-on tail is when you begin the odd- and even-numbered rows. For example,

if you do a long-tail cast-on, your tail will be on the right side of the work at the beginning of odd rows. With Color A, cast on 23 stitches.

ROW 1: Knit 23 stitches.

ROW 2: Knit 15 stitches. You have not finished the row. Turn your work around so the opposite side is facing you.

ROW 3: Slip the first stitch knit-wise from the left-hand needle to the right-hand needle (see page 53). Your yarn should be at the back of the knitting. Knit 6 stitches and turn your work around again. This row begins the shaping of the ball.

ROW 4: With the working yarn at the back of the work, slip the first stitch knitwise. Knit 8 stitches. From this point on, you will work to 2 stitches beyond the gap created by slipping the stitch in the preceding row, then turn the work around.

ROW 5: With the working yarn at the back of the work, slip the first stitch knitwise. Knit 10 stitches, turn.

ROW 6: With the working yarn at the back of the work, slip the first stitch knitwise. Knit 12 stitches, turn.

ROW 7: With the working yarn at the back of the work, slip the first stitch knitwise. Knit 14 stitches, turn.

ROW 8: With the working yarn at the back of the work, slip the first stitch knitwise. Knit 16 stitches, turn.

ROW 9: With the working yarn at the back of the work, slip the first stitch knitwise. Knit 18 stitches, turn.

ROW 10: With the working yarn at the back of the work, slip the first stitch knitwise. Knit 20 stitches (this is the end of the row), turn.

ROW 11: With the working yarn at the back of the work, slip the first stitch knitwise. Knit 22 stitches, turn.

ROW 12: Knit all 23 stitches (without slipping the first stitch as in preceding rows.)

Now change to Color B. Instead of cutting off Color A, carry it up the side of the work, twisting it around Color B whenever the two yarns are at the same side of the piece. (Carrying the unused color in this manner reduces the number of ends you have to weave in later.) Using Color B, repeat rows 1 to 12 for the next section of the ball. Continue to change colors, carrying the unused color up the side, repeat rows 1 to 12 until 10 sections have been knitted—5 of each color. Bind off all stitches, leaving a 15-inch tail of yarn. Using a yarn needle and the tail of yarn, sew the cast-on row to the bind-off row following the Bind Off to Bind Off illustration for the mattress stitch on page 23. Weave the remaining tails through the edge stitches, and use a tail at one side to gather up the stitches along that side and pull tight to close. Leave opposite side open so that you can stuff the ball later.

FELT, STUFF, AND FINISH THE BALL

To felt the unstuffed knitted ball, place it in a pillowcase (or lingerie bag) and tie it shut. Place the pillowcase in your washing machine along with a few old towels (to produce extra agitation and to balance the load) and about one-fourth the amount of laundry detergent you would use for a normal load. Set the machine for a 10-minute hot wash cycle and a cold rinse. When the wash and rinse cycles are complete, check the ball for felting progress. If the knitted stitches have shrunk and adhere to each other and the fabric appears dense and even, with no light shining through it, the felting is complete. If it has not sufficiently felted, return the ball to the pillowcase and washer and repeat the wash and rinse cycles, checking every 1–2 minutes depending on how close your ball is to being completely felted. Felting is not an exact science. The speed at which your ball felts will depend upon the level of agitation in your washing machine, the type of water you have, and the type of detergent you use. It is impossible to reverse the felting process so it is best to tread carefully by checking frequently until you are pleased with your results. When the ball is satisfactorily felted, set it aside to dry.

Stuff the dry ball with clean wool fleece, yarn scraps, or polyester fiberfill until you are happy with the way it feels. Run a strand of yarn around the opening like a drawstring and pull tightly to close. Weave in the ends.

EASY EYELET WASHCLOTH OR BLANKET

MATERIALS

FOR 10-INCH SQUARE BABY WASHCLOTH OR 13-INCH SQUARE ADULT WASHCLOTH

2 skeins Mission Falls 1824 Cotton (50 grams/84 yards; 100% cotton) in ivory #102

1 pair size 5 knitting needles, or size needed to obtain gauge

Yarn needle

FOR 30-INCH SQUARE BLANKET

11 skeins Mission Falls 1824 Cotton (50 grams/84 yards; 100% cotton) in ivory #102

1 size 5 circular needle, 29 inches or longer, or size needed to obtain gauge

Yarn needle

GAUGE

18 stitches and 36 rows = 4 inches on size 5 needles in garter stitch

Whether you make the washcloth (see page 60) or the blanket (see left), you are using the exact same technique: You start with 4 stitches at one corner, then by increasing one stitch at the beginning of every row you build a triangle—the more rows you work and the more stitches you increase, the bigger the triangle. Once you have reached the desired width, you begin decreasing one stitch at the beginning of every row until you have removed almost all the stitches. By working the increases and decreases with yarnovers (explained on page 53), you create a lovely eyelet pattern along the sides. To demonstrate how easily this pattern can be adapted to different types of yarn, we show five versions in the photo on page 61. The main instructions are written for the washcloth and blanket made with Mission Falls Cotton, which is the softest springiest cotton we know and has an appealing knubby texture. The information required to knit the blanket with the other yarns is provided on page 61. Because the blanket requires a lot of stitches, we recommend that you knit it back and forth on circular needles. If you have not done this before, see the instructions on page 36. To take your gauge, we recommend that you make a washcloth.

MAKE FIRST HALF WASHCLOTH/BLANKET

Cast on 4 stitches.

ROW 1: Knit

ROW 2: Knit 2 stitches, increase one stitch by making a yarnover (see page 53), knit to end of row. You now have 5 stitches on your needle.

Repeat Row 2, increasing one stitch, two stitches in from the edge, at the beginning of every row until you have 62 stitches for a baby washcloth, 82 stitches for an adult washcloth, or 189 stitches for a 30-inch blanket. Your knitting is now a triangle shape (half of a square).

MAKE SECOND HALF WASHCLOTH/BLANKET

ROW 1: Knit 1, knit 2 together (see page 53), yarnover, knit 2 together, work to end of row. You have decreased the number of stitches by one. (The first knit 2 together reduces the stitch count; the yarnover continues the decorative edge established in the first half of the piece, and the second knit 2 together cancels out the increase created by the yarnover.) Repeat row 1, decreasing 1 stitch at the beginning of each row until 7 stitches remain.

FINISH WASHCLOTH/ BLANKET

ROW 1: Working with 7 stitches on the needle, knit 2 stitches, slip 1 stitch from the left-hand needle to the right-hand needle without knitting it, knit the next 2 stitches together, then pass the slipped stitch (the second one on the right-hand needle) over the first stitch on the right-hand needle (this is the same action that you perform when you are binding off—see page 19), knit the last 2 stitches. You have decreased 2 stitches so you now have 5 stitches on your needle.

ROW 2: Knit 2 stitches, yarnover, knit 2 together, knit 1—5 stitches remain. Bind off all stitches.

Weave in all loose ends. Block according to instructions on page 24.

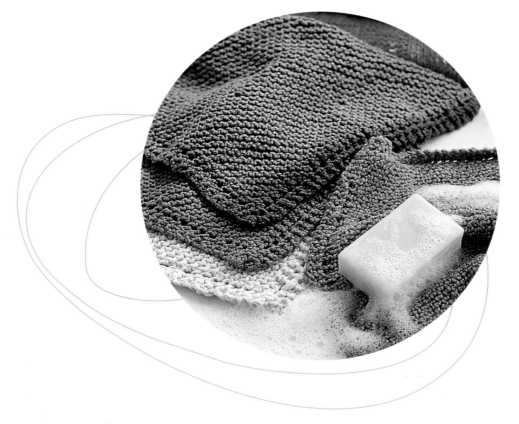

EASY EYELET BLANKET VARIATIONS

While the Easy Eyelet Washcloth is best made in an absorbent cotton, the Easy Eyelet Blanket can be made in virtually any yarn that will feel comfortable next to a baby's skin. Shown here, top to bottom, are blankets made out of Rowan Wool Cotton; Mission Falls 1824 cotton (the same blanket as on page 58); Green Mountain Spinnery Cotton Comfort; Jaeger Matchmaker Merino DK; and Classic Elite La Gran Brushed Mohair. Because some of these yarns knit up at different gauges, the number of stitches you need to make a 30-inch square blanket varies. If you would like to make the blanket in one of these yarns, adapt the pattern based upon the information below.

ROWAN WOOL COTTON
(50% Merino wool, 50% cotton)

Wool makes this blanket warm and elastic; cotton adds to its softness.

To make a 30-inch-square blanket, you will need 8 (50-gram/124-yard) skeins in citrus #901. The gauge is 20 stitches and 40 rows to 4 inches in garter stitch. We recommend size 5 needles or size needed to obtain gauge. Increase to 210 stitches before beginning second half.

GREEN MOUNTAIN SPINNERY COTTON COMFORT
(80% wool, 20% organic cotton)

The organic cotton adds softenss to the fine wool in this yarn, which works up into a soft, lightweight, and durable blanket. The color range has a sublte watercolor appearance, thanks to the cotton, which doesn't take the dye as intensely as the wool.

To make a 30-inch-square blanket, you will need 6 (2-ounce/180-yard) skeins in bluet #6-B. The gauge is 20 stitches and 40 rows to 4 inches in garter stitch. We recommend size 5 needles or size needed to obtain gauge. Increase to 210 stitches before beginning second half.

JAEGER MATCHMAKER MERINO DK
(100% machine-washable wool)

Because this wool yarn is specially treated, this blanket is easy-care. It can be machine-washed and dried.

To make a 30-inch-square blanket, you will need 8 (50-gram/131-yard) skeins in down #863. The gauge is 20 stitches and 40 rows to 4 inches in garter stitch. We recommend size 5 needles or size needed to obtain gauge. Increase to 210 stitches before beginning second half.

CLASSIC ELITE LA GRAN BRUSHED MOHAIR
(76.5% mohair, 17.5% wool, 6% nylon)

This very fluffy and soft mohair makes a fancy blanket, perfect for parties when baby is going to be the center of attention. Mohair is very hard-wearing but needs to be hand-washed.

To make a 30-inch-square blanket, you will need 7 (1$\frac{1}{2}$-ounce/90-yard) skeins in yellow roses #6568. The gauge is 16 stitches and 32 rows to 4 inches in garter stitch. We recommend size 9 needles or size needed to obtain gauge. Increase to 168 stitches before beginning second half.

BEGINNER BOOTIES

SIZE

To fit up to a 3½-inch long foot. If you would like to make smaller or larger booties, change the yarn thickness and needle size.

MATERIALS

1 ball Lane Borgosesia Maratona (50 grams/121 yards; 100% wool), for one pair of booties

Shown in mauve #1399, blue heather #20523, and sage #8533

1 pair size 6 knitting needles, or size needed to obtain gauge

2 size 6 double-pointed needles, for making I-cord tie

Yarn needle

GAUGE

20 stitches and 40 rows = 4 inches on size 6 needles in garter stitch

---

These booties are knitted back and forth on straight needles, starting at the ankle, then down around the foot from ankle to toe. The resulting piece of knitting is then folded and seamed to make a perfect bootie shape. An I-cord tie threaded through eyelet holes around the ankle holds the booties on little feet. The construction may be hard for you to visualize but we guarantee that the instructions are easy to follow once the stitches are on the needles. We chose a very soft merino wool for this project. It is sure to keep baby's feet warm and cozy. Because this project is so small, it doesn't make sense to make a gauge swatch. Instead, start knitting the first bootie and take your gauge after you complete Row 24. We thank our friend Cathy Payson for sharing this pattern with us.

KNIT THE ANKLE

Using the simple cast-on (see page 13), cast on 32 stitches, leaving a 24-inch tail to sew the bootie seam after you have finished knitting. (This cast-on is very stretchy, which will make the booties easy to put on).
ROWS 1–24: Work in garter stitch (knit all stitches), being careful to knit with your working yarn rather than the tail you will use later for seaming. (Note that your cast-on tail is at the end of the row when you are working odd rows, and at the beginning of even rows, through row 27. This will help you to keep track of where you are in the pattern. To count garter rows, count the number of ridges and multiply by 2, as explained on page 25).
ROW 25: Purl all stitches.

ROW 26: Make a row of eyelets (for inserting the tie) as follows: Knit 1, knit 2 together, yarnover (see page 53), knit 1. Repeat this sequence of stitches 7 more times to finish the row.
ROW 27: Purl all stitches.

INCREASE TO BEGIN FOOT SHAPING

ROWS 1 AND 2: Work in garter stitch to end of row, then cast on 3 stitches using the simple cast-on method. At the end of row 2 you will have 38 stitches on your needle. (Note that from this point on in the instructions your cast-on tail is at the beginning of the odd rows and at the end of the even rows.)
ROWS 3–6: Work in garter stitch to end of row, then cast on 2 stitches

MAKING
I-CORD

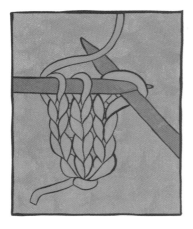

This simple knitted cord is fun and fast to make on two double-pointed needles. Although it is a very old, traditional technique, the late knitting master Elizabeth Zimmermann first gave it the name I-cord in *Knitter's Almanac* (originally published by Charles Scribner's and Sons in 1974, and still in print in a Dover edition).

1. *On one double-pointed needle, cast on the number of stitches called for in the pattern. For the Beginner Baby Booties, cast on 3 stitches. Knit to the end of the row.*

2. *Transfer the needle with the stitches to your left hand, with the working yarn hanging down from the last stitch on the needle. Bring the yarn around behind the work and knit the stitches in the same order again.*

3. *Repeat step 2 until the cord is the length desired. In the beginning it may look like the stitches are bunching up in a knot, but after a few rows you will see a tube of knitting begin to form.*

using the simple cast-on method. At the end of row 6 you will have 46 stitches.

ROWS 7–22: Work in garter stitch.

DECREASE FOR BOTTOM OF SOLE

ROW 1: Knit 2 together 4 times (reducing the first 8 stitches to 4 stitches), knit 7 stitches, knit 2 together 8 times (reducing 16 stitches to 8 stitches), knit 7 stitches, knit 2 together 4 times (reducing 8 stitches to 4 stitches). When you have finished this row, you will have 30 stitches on your needle.

ROWS 2–3: Work in garter stitch. Bind off.

SEW BOOTIE TOGETHER

Fold the bootie in half. Using the mattress stitch and following the Rows to Rows illustration on page 23, sew around the bootie from the top of the ankle around the foot. Following the Bind Off to Bind Off illustration, sew the sole. Weave in ends.

MAKE I-CORD TIE

Cast on 3 stitches on a double-pointed needle and make a 13-inch I-cord following the instructions at left. Thread the I-cord through the eyelets and tie in a bow. Fold the cuff down.

Make another bootie same as the first.

WORKING WITH COLOR IS ONE OF THE MOST EXCITING PARTS
OF KNITTING—WHETHER WORKING A SINGLE-COLOR PROJECT
IN A FAVORITE COLOR, OR WORKING A MULTICOLORED
PROJECT IN A COMBINATION OF COLORS. IN THIS CHAPTER,
WE PRESENT THE MOST COMMON TECHNIQUES FOR WORKING
WITH MORE THAN ONE COLOR—STRIPES, INTARSIA, AND
STRANDED KNITTING—ALL IN SWEATER PROJECTS.

DISCOVERING A NEW
WORLD OF COLOR

chapter 5

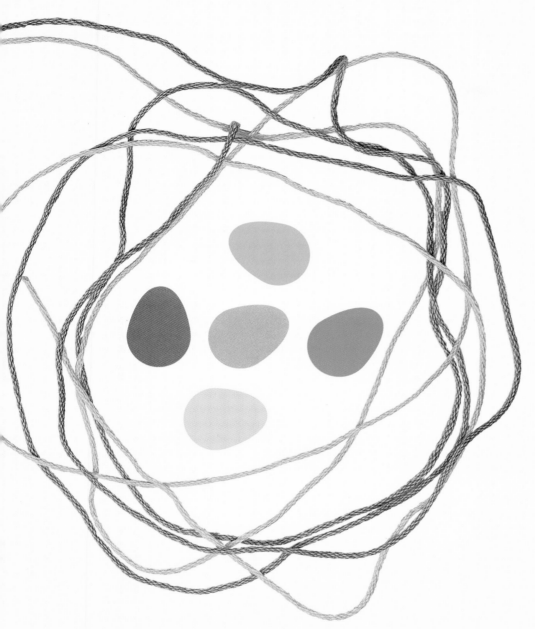

Up to this point, we have written out the instructions for projects in this book in an easy-to-follow style without any of the abbreviations that are standard in most other knitting publications. While we are going to maintain the easy-to-follow part, we will begin to introduce commonly used abbreviations. At the first occurrence in each pattern, we define each abbreviation in parentheses—that way you won't lose any time trying to decipher what we mean but you will still learn what you need to know. In this chapter, we also introduce patterns with multiple sizes. When choosing a size, remember to consider how old or big you expect the baby to be when you finish the project and what season it will be. For example, a wool sweater completed in July should be sized for at least the following fall. For more about sizing, see page 91.

KNITTING AND PLAYING WITH COLOR

Everyone has preconceived notions about color—which colors "go together," can be worn in different seasons, are appropriate for boy and girl babies. Knitting is a fun way to shatter those notions, and to explore and expand your relationship to color. While we, of course, like the colors we chose for the projects in this book, we also hope that you will give these projects your personal stamp by changing them at least some of the time. When you are planning a multicolored project, we suggest that you visit a yarn shop and consider both the colors that you are drawn to naturally and those that you tend to veer away from. See if you might be able to mix and match colors to come up with a new palette, one with which you have never worked and about which you feel excited. To generate new ideas, look at the world around you. Consider borrowing a palette from a favorite painting, the rug beneath your feet, a piece of wrapping paper, or a bird that visits your feeder each morning, anything that catches your eye. If you are unsure as to how your color choices will play out in a project, think about buying sample balls of each color you are considering and playing with them before you commit to the full project purchase. If you are working on a striped project like the Harvard Square Cardigan, "test" your palette by wrapping strands of yarn around a long, narrow piece of cardboard in different orders until you find one that "sings," then follow up with a swatch. For an intarsia project like the Sweetheart Pullover (page 78) or a stranded project like the Nordic Cardigan (page 92), consider sketching the colorwork on knitter's graph paper (sold at yarn stores) in colored pencils that match your yarn colors closely, then swatching small sections. If all the colors are not used equally in the pattern, remember to account for this in your swatch or sketch. While you may love the way equal amounts of a group of colors look lined up next to each other, you may be surprised by how they play out in the pattern. When choosing colors for a baby project, consider the hair color and skin tone of the baby (if known), the style of the parents (since moms and dads are not likely to dress their babies in clothes they don't like), and the colors that are going to satisfy you and are going to keep you knitting happily.

STRIPED KNITTING

There's nothing tricky about working with stripes. At the introduction of a new color, you simply tie on the new yarn as explained on page 33. Once a color is introduced into the stripe sequence, you can carry it up the side of the garment so that it will be available when you need it again (instructions for this are given in our patterns). Twist the unused yarns around the working yarn every few rows to secure the loose strands and help maintain tension on the carried yarns so the edge stitches don't become loose.

INTARSIA

Intarsia is the technique employed when you want to work large patches of a color in a specific section of a garment, such as the plum-colored heart in the center of the terracotta Sweetheart Pullover on page 78. Rather than carrying both colors across the entire row (which is what you do in stranded knitting), you use separate balls of yarn for each area and, on the wrong side of the fabric, firmly twist the colors around each other where they meet (if the twist isn't firm, you will have a little hole in the fabric where the colors change). For example, when you are knitting the Sweetheart Pullover, begin with one ball of yarn and work as you normally would until the heart begins. At that point, join a ball of yarn in the heart color and work the first heart stitch, then join another ball of the background color and work to the end of the row. Don't forget to twist the yarns around each other at the color changes. When you turn your knitting to work back on the wrong side, the ends of the working yarns will be waiting for you when you get to the color changes. To avoid tangles, consider working with shorter pieces of yarn, about 3–4 feet long, instead of full balls. The illustration here shows how two colors of yarn are twisted around each other at the point of the color change on the wrong side of the work.

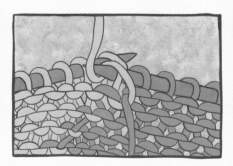

STRANDED KNITTING

Stranding is the technique employed when two or more colors are worked in a repeating pattern sequence over a small number of stitches (usually 5 or fewer), such as in the Nordic Cardigan on page 92. It is also known as Fair Isle knitting, after an island in the North Sea famous for garments made using this technique. To work a stranded project, on the first row where a new color is introduced, work until the new color is needed, then drop the old color, pick up the new color, bring it up from underneath the dropped color and knit with it. When it is time to switch back to the first color, drop the second color, then pick up the first color and bring it under the dropped color. The strands of yarn carried across the back are called floats. Be careful to carry the floats so they lay flat against the work. They shouldn't hang down in loops or be so tight that the work puckers. The illustrations here show how the floats are carried when working on the knit and purl sides of a project.

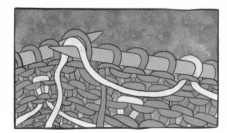

3 months, 6 months, 9 months, 12 months, 18 months, 24 months

Finished chest circumference, buttoned: 19 (20^1/2, 23, 25, 28, 30)"

Both sweaters shown in size 12 months

MATERIALS

FOR SOLID-COLOR CARDIGAN:
2 (3, 3, 4, 4, 5) skeins
Classic Elite Yarns Waterspun Felted
Merino Wool (50 grams/137 yards;
100% wool) in faded rose #5025

FOR STRIPED CARDIGAN:
1 (2, 2, 2, 3, 3) skeins bisque #5087–
referred to as Color A in the pattern

1 (1, 1, 2, 2, 2) skeins gray #5075–
referred to as Color B in the pattern

1 (1, 1, 2, 2, 2) skeins teal #5072–
referred to as Color C in the pattern

FOR BOTH VERSIONS:
29-inch circular needles in size 6,
or size needed to obtain gauge

29-inch circular needles in size 8,
or size needed to obtain gauge

Four ^{5}/8" buttons

2 stitch holders

Yarn needle

T-pins

Scrap yarn, removable stitch markers,
or rustproof coil-less safety pins

GAUGE

18 sts and 36 rows = 4" in garter
stitch using larger needles

The body of this sweater (the two fronts and the back) is worked in one piece up to the armholes. At that point, the work is divided and the different sections (the fronts, the back, and the sleeves) are worked separately. After all of the seams are sewn, a garter-stitch border is added to correct any unevenness in the knitting along the edges. This sweater can be worked in stripes, as shown at left, or in a solid color, as shown on page 73. The accompanying Garter Stitch Cloche gets its cloche (bell) shape from short-row shaping, the same technique used for Baby's First Ball on page 55. The cloche pattern begins on page 76.

CHOOSE SIZE

This pattern includes six sizes. The first number given refers to size 3 months, and the numbers in parentheses refer to sizes 6 months, 9 months, 12 months, 18 months, and 24 months, in that order. To make it easier to follow the instructions, choose the size you want and go through the pattern and highlight all of the numbers that apply to that size. If you do not want to write directly in the book, photocopy the instructions and highlight the copy.

MAKE A GAUGE SWATCH

Using larger needles, cast on 22 stitches and work in garter stitch for approximately 5". Block the swatch the way you intend to block the finished sweater (see page 24).

Measure your gauge over a 4-inch square section of the swatch. It is important that you match both the stitch gauge and row gauge.

BEGIN SWEATER BODY

With larger needles (and Color C if you are making the striped sweater), CO (cast on) 86 (92, 104, 113, 126, 135) sts (stitches). Work in garter stitch (knit all stitches in all rows), following the color sequence on page 74 if you are making the striped sweater, until the piece meas (measures) ^{3}/4".

MAKE A YARNOVER BUTTONHOLE

Buttonholes and shaping instructions in knitting patterns often refer to the right (public) and wrong (inside face) sides of the work.

BUTTONHOLE PLACEMENT

The buttonholes for this sweater are worked as you knit the fronts, rather than in a separate button-hole band. To determine the correct spacing for the sweater size you are making, refer to the chart below. Make the buttonholes where indicated as you work through the pattern for the sweater body.

SIZE	1ST BH	2ND BH	3RD BH	4TH BH
Size 3 Months	3/4"	3"	5"	7 1/4"
Size 6 Months	3/4"	3 1/4"	5 3/4"	8 1/4"
Size 9 Months	3/4"	3 1/2"	6 1/4"	9"
Size 12 Months	3/4"	3 3/4"	6 3/4"	10"
Size 18 Months	3/4"	4"	7 1/2"	10 3/4"
Size 24 Months	3/4"	4 1/2"	8"	11 3/4"

Solid-color garter-stitch knitting looks the same on both sides, so if you are making the solid-color sweater, you will need to choose one side to be the right side. To do this, hold your knitting as if you were ready to work the next row and mark the side that's facing you as the right side with a yarn tie or a coil-less safety pin.

To make the first set of buttonholes, one on both the right and left fronts, k4 (knit 4 sts), yo (yarnover; see page 53), k2tog (knit 2 together; see page 53), knit until there are 6 sts left, k2tog, yo, k4. Your buttonholes are complete. On the next row, knit all stitches as usual in garter stitch, including the yarnovers. Refer to the chart above to find out where the remaining three buttonholes should be placed. Work the buttonhole row whenever the work measures the length indicated as you con-

tinue through the remainder of the pattern. If you want to make a cardigan with buttonholes on only one front, make each buttonhole at the beginning of the row for a girl, or at the end of the row for a boy.

Continue knitting in garter stitch, placing buttonholes as indicated on the chart until piece measures 4 1/2 (5 , 5 1/2, 6, 6 1/2, 7)", ending after you have completed a WS (wrong-side) row. On the next row, divide the work at the armholes into two fronts and a back as follows: Work 22 (23, 26, 28, 32, 34) sts for right front, slip these stitches to a holder, work next 42 (46, 52, 57, 62, 67) sts for the back, drop the working yarn, and slip the remaining 22 (23, 26, 28, 32, 34) sts for the left front to another holder. Resume working on the back stitches only until the piece meas 9 (10, 11, 12, 13, 14)" from the beginning. BO (bind off) all sts.

FINISH RIGHT FRONT

Transfer the 22 (23, 26, 28, 32, 34) sts for the right front (the first stitches you put on a holder) to your knitting needle. Join a new ball of yarn at the armhole edge and work in garter stitch, placing buttonholes as necessary, until piece meas 7 1/2 (8 1/2, 9 1/4, 10 1/4, 11, 12)" and you are ready to work a RS (right-side) row (center front edge of cardigan). All the buttonholes should have been completed by now. On next row, to begin shaping the neckline, bind off 10 (10, 10, 11, 11, 12) sts at beginning of the row, then work to the end of the row. Turn and work back across the remaining 12 (13, 16, 17, 21, 22) sts. Turn work. You are now at center front edge again. Decrease 1 stitch by knitting first 2 sts together, then work to end of row. Knit the next WS (wrong-side) row even (without any shaping). Continue to decrease at the beginning of the RS rows (center front edge) 4 more times for a total of 5 decreases. When you finish your decreases, you will have 7 (8, 11, 12, 16, 17) sts on your needles. Work even on these stitches until the right front measures the same as the back—9 (10, 11, 12, 13, 14)". BO all shoulder stitches.

FINISH LEFT FRONT

Transfer the 22 (23, 26, 28, 32, 34) sts for the left front (the only stitches on a holder at this point) to your knitting needle. Join a new ball of yarn at the armhole edge, ready to work a RS row, and work in garter stitch, placing the buttonholes, as necessary, until piece meas 7 1/2 (8 1/2, 9 1/4, 10 1/4, 11, 12)" and you are ready to work a WS row. All the buttonholes should have been completed by now. On next row, to begin shaping the neckline, bind off 10 (10, 10, 11, 11, 12) sts at beginning of the row, then work to the end of the row. Turn and work back across the rem (remaining) 12 (13, 16, 17, 21, 22) sts. Turn work. You are now at the center front edge again. Decrease 1 stitch by knitting first 2 sts together, then work to end of row. Knit the next RS row even. Continue to decrease at the beginning of the WS rows (center front edge) 4 more times for a total of 5 decreases. When you finish your

decreases, you will have 7 (8, 11, 12, 16, 17) sts on your needles. Work even on these stitches until the left front measures the same as the back and right front—9 (10, 11, 12, 13, 14)". BO all shoulder stitches.

MAKE SLEEVES

With smaller circular needle, CO 23 (25, 25, 27, 27, 29) sts and work in garter stitch for 1 1/2". You are using the smaller needles so that the cuffs of the sweater draw in slightly and will fit snugly. Change to the larger needle (simply knit the stitches from the smaller needle onto the larger needle) and, on the first stitch, increase 1 by knitting into the front and the back of the same stitch (see page 52). Knit to the last stitch in the row and increase 1 stitch by knitting into the front and back of the last stitch. You now have 25 (27, 27, 29, 29, 31) stitches on the needle. Continue working in garter stitch, increasing 1 stitch at each end of the row every 4th row 8 (9, 11, 13, 15, 16) more times. When you finish your increases, you should have 41 (45, 49, 55, 59, 63) sts on your needles. Work even (without further shaping) in garter stitch until the sleeve meas 6 1/2 (7, 7 1/2, 8 1/2, 10, 11)". BO all sts. Make a second sleeve same as the first.

BUTTONS & GENDER

Traditionally, girls' cardigans have buttonholes on the right front and boys' cardigans have buttonholes on the left front. To make this sweater unisex (so it can be passed from sibling to sibling and generation to generation), buttonholes are worked on both fronts. The buttons, sewn on top of the unused buttonholes, can be moved from one side to the other as necessary. If you are making this sweater in a very small size and are worried about the buttons as a choking hazard, skip the buttonholes and buttons completely.

Weave in the ends on body and sleeves of the sweater using a yarn needle. Sew the shoulder seams following illustration on page 23 for Bind Off to Bind Off on garter stitch. Sew the sleeve seams following the illustration for sewing Rows to Rows on garter stitch. Sew the sleeves into the armhole opening as follows: Using T-pins, pin the sleeve seam to the bottom of the armhole (where you divided the body into fronts and back). Pin the midpoint of the top of the sleeve to the shoulder seam. Gently stretch both open edges and place another pin halfway down on each side to attach each sleeve to the body. These 4 pins will give you a guideline for making the seam as smooth as possible.

Sew the sleeve into the armhole following the illustration labeled Rows to Bind Off, skipping every other row because in garter stitch there are just about twice as many rows as stitches. Your own judgment is the best tool for making neat seams. Look at your work, and be prepared to undo and redo a section of the seam if the pieces aren't going together smoothly. While you are sewing, be sure to pull along the length of the seam firmly to stretch out the sewn stitches so they lie flat. If the stitches are too tight, they will pucker.

STRIPED SWEATER

If you are making the striped sweater, follow the pattern as written, changing colors every 2 rows as follows:

COLOR SEQUENCE

ROWS 1 AND 2: WORK IN COLOR C.

ROWS 3 AND 4: WORK IN COLOR A.

ROWS 5 AND 6: WORK IN COLOR B.

ROWS 7 AND 8: WORK IN COLOR A.

Repeat these 8 rows throughout for color pattern. Finish as for the solid version, sewing the seams at the top of the sleeves and the shoulders with matching yarn color. For the sleeve seams, where you will be working up the side of the striped fabric, use the darkest color for the entire seam because it will be less noticeable. Use Color C for edging.

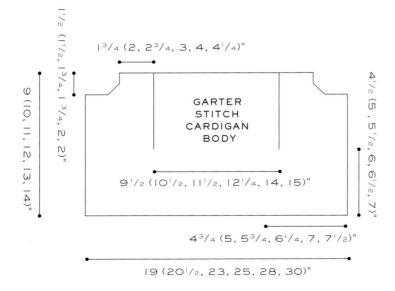

GARTER STITCH CARDIGAN BODY

$1^{3}/_{4}$ (2, $2^{3}/_{4}$, 3, 4, $4^{1}/_{4}$)"

$1^{1}/_{2}$ ($1^{1}/_{2}$, $1^{3}/_{4}$, $1^{3}/_{4}$, 2, 2)"

9 (10, 11, 12, 13, 14)"

$4^{1}/_{2}$ (5, $5^{1}/_{2}$, 6, $6^{1}/_{2}$, 7)"

$9^{1}/_{2}$ ($10^{1}/_{2}$, $11^{1}/_{2}$, $12^{1}/_{4}$, 14, 15)"

$4^{3}/_{4}$ (5, $5^{3}/_{4}$, $6^{1}/_{4}$, 7, $7^{1}/_{2}$)"

19 ($20^{1}/_{2}$, 23, 25, 28, 30)"

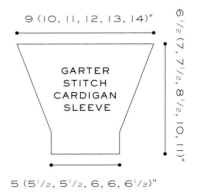

GARTER STITCH CARDIGAN SLEEVE

9 (10, 11, 12, 13, 14)"

$6^{1}/_{2}$ (7, $7^{1}/_{2}$, $8^{1}/_{2}$, 10, 11)"

5 ($5^{1}/_{2}$, $5^{1}/_{2}$, 6, 6, $6^{1}/_{2}$)"

MAKE GARTER STITCH EDGING

Starting at the lower right front corner, with the RS of the work facing you, pick up and knit a one-row border around the entire cardigan (see illustration at right) as follows: 34 (38, 41, 46, 49, 54) sts from bottom edge to beginning of neck shaping (approximately 1 stitch for every garter ridge), 17 (17, 18, 19, 20, 20) sts from beginning of neck shaping to right shoulder seam, 27 sts across the back of the neck to left shoulder seam, 17 (17, 18, 19, 20, 20) sts from left shoulder seam to beginning of neck shaping, and 34 (38, 41, 46, 49, 54) sts from neck shaping to bottom left front corner—129 (137, 145, 157, 165, 175) stitches. Turn

your work around so you are ready to work a WS row. BO neatly. It is especially important to work the bind-off neatly with an even tension because the center front edge is a focal point of the garment. Block according to instructions on page 24.

SEW ON BUTTONS

Overlap the 2 fronts with the side where you want the buttonholes to be on top, making sure the neck and bottom edges are even. Using a large pin and working on a flat surface, open each buttonhole slightly, and, working through the hole, mark the button position on the layer of fabric underneath, about 1" in from the center front edge of the cardigan. Sew a button at each marked position.

PICKING UP STITCHES FOR GARTER-STITCH EDGING

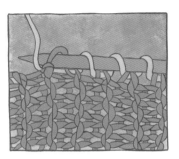

To pick up and knit stitches along a garter-stitch edge, as for the edging on the Garter Stitch Cardigan, starting at the lower right front corner, insert the needle into the center of the first edge stitch from front to back, wrap the working yarn around the needle, and pull up a loop as for an ordinary knit stitch so the newly wrapped yarn becomes the first stitch on the right-hand needle. Insert the needle into the stitches between the garter ridges, in other words, into every other row of the garment edge. On bound-off edges, pick up approximately 1 stitch per bound-off stitch, or as instructed in pattern.

GARTER STITCH CLOCHE

FINISHED SIZE

17-inch circumference,
one size fits up to 24 months

MATERIALS

Classic Elite Waterspun Felted
Merino Wool (50 grams/
137 yards; 100% wool)

1 skein faded rose #5025,
bisque #5087, or teal #5072

1 pair size 8 needles, or size
needed to obtain gauge

Yarn needle

GAUGE

18 stitches and 36 rows = 4 inches
on size 8 needles in garter stitch

A version of this little cloche was published "for cyclers" in a 19th-century knitting book. To help keep track of your place in the pattern, take note of where your cast-on tail is when you are working odd and even rows. For example, if you use a long-tail cast-on, the tail will be at the beginning of the needle when you are ready to work a right-side row. You might also use a row counter and/or check off the rows as you complete them. In addition, once you begin the shaping in row 22, mark the beginning edge of your work and always remember that the shaping happens at the opposite end of the row (at the crown). Because this hat is so small, it doesn't make sense to do a true gauge swatch. Instead, simply start knitting the hat. After you have finished a few inches, measure your gauge. If it is correct, continue knitting. If it isn't, determine whether you want to start over with a different size needle. The pattern will work even if you're not knitting exactly to the recommended gauge, although you should try to be fairly close.

Cast on 20 stitches.

ROW 1: Knit all stitches.

ROW 2: Knit to last stitch. Increase 1 stitch by knitting into the front and back of the last stitch (see page 52). You now have 21 stitches on your needle.

ROW 3: Knit all stitches.

ROW 4: Knit to last stitch. Increase 1 stitch by knitting into the front and back of the last stitch. You now have 22 stitches on your needle. You will continue this increase at the end of each even-numbered row through Row 20, but from now on the pattern will be written in a convenient shorthand.

ROW 5: K22. (In other words, knit 22 stitches or knit all stitches on your needle.)

ROW 6: Knit 21, inc 1 in last st—23 stitches. (In other words, knit to last stitch. Increase 1 stitch by knitting into the front and back of the last stitch. You now have 23 stitches on your needle.)

ROW 7: K23.

ROW 8: K22, inc 1 in last st—24 sts.

ROW 9: K24.

ROW 10: K23, inc 1 in last st—25 sts.

ROW 11: K25.

ROW 12: K24, inc 1 in last st—26 sts.

ROW 13: K26.

ROW 14: K25, inc 1 in last st—27 sts.

ROW 15: K27.

ROW 16: K26, inc 1 in last st—28 sts.

ROW 17: K28.

ROW 18: K28, inc 1 in last st—29 sts.

ROW 19: K29.

ROW 20: K29, inc 1 in last st—30 sts.

ROW 21: K30. You have completed the set-up section of your hat, which looks like a trapezoid. You will now start knitting the six main "pie" sections of your hat.

ROW 22: K20. Leave 10 stitches not worked on your left needle. Turn your work so that the opposite side is facing you.

ROW 23: With the working yarn in front of your work, slip 1 stitch from the left needle to the right needle as if to purl, pass the working yarn between the needles to the back of the work, k19 to end of row.

ROW 24: K21. (You are knitting to 1 stitch beyond the gap created when you slipped a stitch on the previous row.). Turn your work so the opposite side is facing you.

ROW 25: Sl 1, k20 (In other words, with the working yarn in front of your work, slip 1 stitch as you did in row 23, then, with your working yarn in back of your work, knit 20 to end of row.)

ROW 26: K22, turn.

ROW 27: Sl 1, k21.

ROW 28: K23, turn.

ROW 29: Sl 1, k22.

ROW 30: K24, turn.

ROW 31: Sl 1, k23.

ROW 32: K25, turn.

ROW 33: Sl 1, k24.

ROW 34: K26, turn.

ROW 35: Sl 1, K25.

ROW 36: K27, turn.

ROW 37: Sl 1, k26.

ROW 38: K28, turn.

ROW 39: Sl 1, K27.

ROW 40: K29, turn.

ROW 41: Sl 1, k28.

ROW 42: K30, turn.

ROW 43: Sl 1, k29.

You have completed the first main "pie" section of your hat. Repeat rows 22 through 43 five more times so you finish with 1 set-up section and 6 main "pie" sections. (NOTE: Pretty quickly you'll be able to work this project without looking at the instructions; beware, however, that it's very easy to forget row 43 after knitting the 30 stitches of row 42. If you forget row 43, when you return to row 22 to knit the next pie section you might make the mistake of working your shaping on the wrong end of the hat—on the bottom border instead of the crown). BO (bind off), leaving a tail about 15 inches long.

Starting at the unshaped edge, using a yarn needle, sew the bind-off stitches to the cast-on stitches using the mattress stitch until the cast-on stitches are used up (see page 23). From this point on, sew the bind-off edge to shaped edge of the set-up section, ending at the top of the crown.

SWEETHEART PULLOVER

This pullover is the most basic of sweater shapes (that means it is super-easy to knit). There is no special stitch used for the bottom, sleeve, or neckband; instead, the stockinette stitch is left to curl, which it does naturally, and the curl becomes a design feature. If you are up for a small challenge, make this sweater with an intarsia heart (as shown at left) or a seed stitch heart (as shown on page 80). Or keep it simple and make it in a solid color as shown on page 82.

SIZES

3 months, 6 months,
9 months, 12 months,
18 months, 24 months

Finished chest circumference:
18 (20, 22, 24, 26, 28)"

All sweaters shown
in size 12 months

MATERIALS

Jo Sharp Wool (50 grams/
107 yards; 100% wool)

For Solid-Color Pullover:
3 (3, 4, 4, 5, 5) skeins citrus #509

For Intarsia Heart Pullover:
3 (3, 4, 4, 5, 5) skeins terracotta
#332 and 1 skein plum #505

For Seed Stitch Heart Pullover:
3 (3, 4, 4, 5, 5) skeins pistachio
#002

FOR ALL VERSIONS:
1 pair size 4 needles, or size
needed to obtain gauge

1 pair size 6 needles, or size
needed to obtain gauge

Stitch markers

Stitch holders

Yarn needle

T-Pins

GAUGE

18 stitches and 24 rows = 4"
in stockinette stitch using
larger needles

CHOOSE SIZE
Select a size as instructed on page 71.

MAKE A GAUGE SWATCH
Using larger needles, cast on 24 stitches and work in St st (stockinette stitch; knit 1 row, purl 1 row, repeat) for approximately 5 inches. Block the swatch as you intend to block the finished sweater (see page 24). Measure your gauge over a 4-inch square section of the swatch.

MAKE BACK
With smaller needles, CO (cast on) 41 (45, 49, 53, 59, 63) sts (stitches). Work in St st for 2". Change to larger needles by working the next row onto the new needles. Work in St st until piece meas (measures) 11 (12, 13, 14, 15, 16)", and end having just completed a WS (wrong-side) row. On the next row, BO (bind off) the first 10 (12, 13, 15, 17, 18) sts, knit the next 21 (21, 23, 23, 25, 27) sts, slip the stitches just worked to a holder, BO the rem (remaining) 10 (12, 13, 15, 17, 18) sts.

MAKE FRONT
If you are making the solid-color sweater, work same as back until piece meas 8 1/2 (9 1/2, 10 1/2, 11 1/2, 12 1/2, 13 1/2)", ending after you have completed a WS row, then proceed to the instructions for Shape Front Neck. If you are making the sweater with a seed stitch or intarsia heart, work same as back until piece meas 3 1/4 (4, 4 3/4, 4, 4 3/4, 5 1/4)", ending after you have completed a WS row. Beg (begin) working heart motif following the chart for your size on page 81. For first row, K9 (11, 13, 15, 18, 20), pm (place marker). If you are making the 3-, 6-, or 9-month size, work small heart motif over center 23 sts, then place a second marker and knit last 9 (11, 13) sts of row. If you are making the 12-, 18-, or 24-month size, work

large heart motif over center 23 sts, then place a second marker and knit last 15 (18, 20) sts of row. (The markers are an aid to help you see where the sts for the chart pattern begin and end. When you come to a marker, just slip it from the left needle to the right needle and continue.) On the next row after the chart is finished, remove the markers as you come to them, and continue working in St st across all sts. Continue in St st until piece meas 8¹/2 (9¹/2, 10¹/2, 11¹/2, 12¹/2, 13¹/2)", ending after you have completed a WS row.

SHAPE FRONT NECK
Work 14 (16, 17, 19, 21, 22) sts (these will be the left shoulder edge as the sweater is worn), slip center 13 (13, 15, 15, 17, 19) sts to holder (these are the center front neck sts), join a second ball of yarn, and work the rem 14 (16, 17, 19, 21, 22) sts to end (these are the right shoulder sts when worn). Now you will work only on the sts for the right shoulder. The sts for the left shoulder will stay on the needle, but you will ignore them for now. Working only on the sts for the right shoulder, where your second ball of yarn is connected, turn the work around and purl 14 (16, 17, 19, 21, 22) sts. Turn again, BO 1 st at the beginning of the next RS (right-side) row, and knit to the end of the row—13 (15, 16, 18, 20, 21) sts rem. Continue in this manner, working a WS row, then a RS row

with 1 st BO at the beginning of the row, until there are 10 (12, 13, 15, 17, 18) sts rem for this shoulder. Work even (without further shaping), until piece meas the same as back. BO this group of sts. Now you will work on the sts for the other side, using the first ball of yarn, which is still connected to the left shoulder sts. Turn the work, BO 1 st at the beginning of the next WS row, purl to end—13 (15, 16, 18, 20, 21) sts. Turn again and knit across all sts. Continue to BO 1 st at the beginning of each WS row, work to end, then work a RS row without shaping, until 10 (12, 13, 15, 17, 18) sts rem. Work even until this shoulder measures the

same as the other side. BO this group of sts. (Because you can only BO sts at the beginning of a row, neck shaping is worked by BO sts at the beginning of RS rows for one side, and at the beginning of WS rows for the other side.)

MAKE SLEEVES
With smaller needles, cast on 23 (23, 25, 25, 27, 29) sts. Work in St st for 1¹/2", ending after you have completed a WS row. Change to larger needles and beg increasing to shape sleeve. (If you make your increases inside the selvedge (edge) sts at each side, your work will have neater selvedges, and it will be easier

TIPS FOR KNITTING FROM CHARTS

Charts are common in knitting instructions, especially when you are doing intarsia, stranded knitting, and some texture work. They effectively communicate not only what you are supposed to do, but also what the result will look like—think of them as road maps. Each square on a chart represents a stitch as it appears when viewed from the right side of the work. The squares are either filled in with a color (to represent a color of yarn) or a symbol (to represent either a color or a particular type of stitch). Unless otherwise noted, the odd-numbered rows are RS (right-side) rows and are read from right to left; the even-numbered rows are WS (wrong-side) rows and are read from left to right. If you are having trouble reading and/or keeping your place on the chart, consider the following helpful techniques:

• *Make an enlarged photocopy of the chart and mark off each row as it is completed.*

• *Place a ruler just above the row you are working, so you can see how the new row relates to what you've already done.*

• *Use a clear magnifying ruler to keep track of the row you're on.*

• *Persuade a friend to read the chart aloud to you!*

HEART CHARTS

Below are the charts you need to make the Sweetheart Pullover with either a seed stitch or intarsia heart. For the intarsia heart, you change colors as indicated using the intarsia technique explained on page 69. For the seed stitch heart, you alternate knit and purl stitches to create the bas relief texture. On right-side rows, work chart from right to left (stitch 1–23); on wrong-side rows, work from left to right (stitch 23–1).

USE THESE CHARTS FOR SIZES 3, 6, AND 9 MONTHS: HEART MOTIF OVER 23 STS AND 25 ROWS

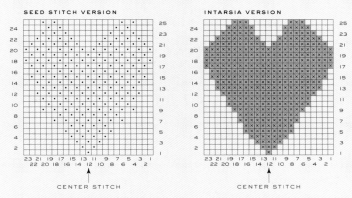

HEART WILL MEASURE ABOUT 5" WIDE AND 4⅛" HIGH.

USE THESE CHARTS FOR SIZES 12, 18, AND 24 MONTHS: HEART MOTIF OVER 23 STS AND 34 ROWS

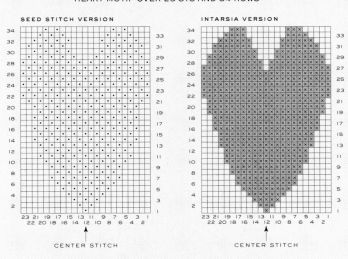

HEART WILL MEASURE ABOUT 5" WIDE AND 5⅔" HIGH.

KEY FOR SEED STITCH HEART

☐ KNIT ON RS OF WORK, PURL ON WS OF WORK

⊡ PURL ON RS OF WORK, KNIT ON WS OF WORK

KEY FOR INTARSIA HEART

☐ IN MAIN COLOR, KNIT ON RS OF WORK, PURL ON WS OF WORK

☒ IN CONTRAST COLOR, KNIT ON RS OF WORK, PURL ON WS OF WORK

PICKING UP STOCKINETTE STITCHES FOR NECKBAND

To pick up and knit stitches for the neckband of the Sweetheart Pullover, with the RS facing, knit the number of stitches given in the instructions from the back neck holder. Referring to the illustration and the instructions, pick up and knit 1 stitch in the left shoulder seam by inserting the right-hand needle from RS to WS into the seam stitch, wrapping yarn around the needle as for knitting a stitch, and pulling a loop through (1 st picked up and knit). Pick up and knit the remainder of the stitches for the left side of the neck as follows: On the vertical section of the neck (the part worked with no shaping), working one full stitch in from the edge, pick up 3 stitches for every 4 rows—this means *pick up 1 stitch in each of the first 3 rows going down the side of the neck toward the center front, then skip 1 row; rep from * as

needed. On the shaped section (the part where the BO stitches were worked), pick up 1 stitch in each row. Knit the stitches from front neck holder, then pick up and knit stitches along right neck edge. Be sure that you pick up the same number on the right neck edge as on the left neck edge, and in approximately the same area. Otherwise, the neckband may not be symmetrical.

When picking up and knitting stitches for a front band, as for the Nordic Cardigan (page 92), work as given above, except on the center front and other vertical sections, pick up and knit approximately 3 stitches for every 4 rows; for shaped section of the neck, pick up 1 stitch for each row.

to sew the seams together.) On the next RS row, knit 1, increase 1 by knitting into the front and back of the next st (see page 52), knit to last 2 sts, increase 1 by knitting into the front and back of the next st, end knit 1—25 (25, 27, 27, 29, 31) sts. Purl across the next row. Continue to work in this manner, increasing 1 st at each side every other row (increase on RS row, then purl across 1 WS row without shaping, repeat), until you have increased 1 st at each side 4 (4, 4, 5, 5, 5) more times, ending having just worked a WS row, to finish with 33 (33, 35, 37, 39, 41) sts. Now increase 1 st at each side every 4th row (by increasing on a RS row as before, then working

3 rows without shaping), a total of 5 (6, 7, 7, 8, 9) times, to finish with 43 (45, 49, 51, 55, 59) sts. Work even until piece meas 7 (7 1/2, 8 1/2, 9 1/2, 10, 11)". BO all sts. Make a second sleeve the same as the first.

SEW ONE SHOULDER SEAM

Using the mattress stitch and following the Bind Off to Bind Off illustration on page 23, sew the front and back together at the left shoulder seam (which will be to the right of the neck opening when you are looking at the front of the sweater).

FINISH NECKLINE & SEW SECOND SHOULDER SEAM

With the RS of the work facing you and using smaller needles, begin at right back neck where shoulder seam ended and pick up 60 (60, 64, 64, 68, 72) sts around neck opening as shown on page 82 and as follows: Pick up and knit 21 (21, 23, 23, 25, 27) sts from back neck holder, 13 sts from left shoulder seam to front holder, 13 (13, 15, 15, 17, 19) sts from front neck holder, 13 sts from holder to right shoulder. Purl the next row on WS. Working back and forth in St st as established, work 4 more rows, and end having just worked a WS row. Now decrease to make the neckline a little more snug as follows: *K6, k2tog; repeat from * 7 (7, 8, 8, 8, 9) times, end k4 (4, 0, 0, 4, 0), to

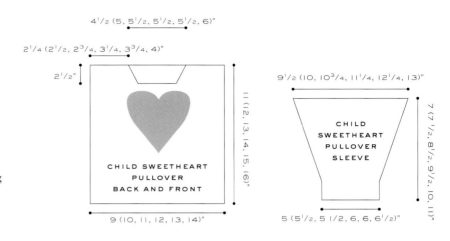

4 1/2 (5, 5 1/2, 5 1/2, 5 1/2, 6)"

2 1/4 (2 1/2, 2 3/4, 3 1/4, 3 3/4, 4)"

2 1/2"

11 (12, 13, 14, 15, 16)"

CHILD SWEETHEART PULLOVER BACK AND FRONT

9 (10, 11, 12, 13, 14)"

9 1/2 (10, 10 3/4, 11 1/4, 12 1/4, 13)"

7 (7 1/2, 8 1/2, 9 1/2, 10, 11)"

CHILD SWEETHEART PULLOVER SLEEVE

5 (5 1/2, 5 1/2, 6, 6, 6 1/2)"

finish with 53 (53, 56, 56, 60, 63) sts (see illustration for k2tog on page 53). Continue working in St st until piece measures 3" from the pick-up row. BO all sts loosely but neatly. (You may find it helpful to use the larger size needle for working the BO row to assure that sweater will fit over baby's head easily.) Sew the other shoulder and neckband seam.

SEW IN SLEEVES

Lay the sweater out flat, right side up, with the neck opening in the middle, and the front and back extending above and below it. Place removable markers or pins 4 3/4 (5, 5 1/2, 5 3/4, 6 1/8, 6 1/2)" from the shoulder seam along each side of the front and back. Fold each sleeve in half the long way and mark the midpoint of the top edge of the sleeve. Pin the sleeve to the body

between the markers at front and back, matching the midpoint sleeve marker to the shoulder seam. Sew the top of the sleeve to the body using the mattress stitch illustration labeled Rows to Bind Off (see page 23). As you work, tug along the length of the seam to stretch out the sewn stitches so that the seam will lie flat.

SEW SLEEVE AND SIDE SEAMS

With wrong sides of the garment together, pin the long seam from the bottom edge of the body to the sleeve cuff, matching the ends and the point where the sleeves join the body at the underarm. Place pins 1"–2" apart. Using the mattress stitch (see page 45), sew sleeve and side seams, removing pins as you work. Weave in loose ends. Block according to instructions on page 24.

ADULT SWEETHEART PULLOVER

This casual unisex sweater is a classic for men and women. It looks exactly like the baby sweater minus the heart.

MAKE GAUGE SWATCH
Follow instructions given for child's sweater on page 79.

MAKE BACK
With smaller needles, CO (cast on) 91 (99, 109, 117) stitches (sts). Work in St st (stockinette stitch; knit 1 row, purl 1 row, repeat) for 3", uncurling the fabric to meas (measure) from the cast-on edge. Change to larger needles and work in St st until piece meas 25 (26, 27, 28)", ending having finished a WS (wrong side) row. On the next row, BO (bind off) the first 31 (34, 38, 41) sts, knit the next 29 (31, 33, 35) sts. Slip the sts just worked to a holder, BO the rem (remaining) 31 (34, 38, 41) sts.

MAKE FRONT
Work same as back until piece meas 22 1/2 (23 1/2, 24 1/2, 25 1/2)" from beginning, ending after you have completed a WS (wrong-side) row. Shape front neck as follows: work 35 (38, 42, 45) stitches (these will be the left shoulder edge as the sweater is worn), slip center 21 (23, 25, 27) stitches to holder (these are the center front neck stitches), join a second ball of yarn, and work the remaining 35 (38, 42, 45) stitches to end (these are the right shoulder stitches when worn). Working only on the sts for the right shoulder, where your second ball of yarn is connected, turn the work around and purl 35 (38, 42, 45) sts. Turn again, BO 1 st at the beginning of the next RS (right-side) row, and knit to the end of the row—34 (37, 41, 44) sts. Continue in this manner, working a WS row, then a RS row with 1 st BO at the beginning of the RS row, until there are 31 (34, 38, 41) sts for this shoulder. Work even (without further shaping), until piece meas the same as back. BO this group of sts. Now you will work on the sts for the other side, using the first ball of yarn, which is still connected to the left shoulder sts. Turn the work, BO 1 st at the beginning of the next WS row, purl to end—34 (37, 41, 44) sts. Turn again and knit across all sts. Continue to BO 1 st at the beginning of each WS row, work to end, then work a RS row without shaping, until there are 31 (34, 38, 41) sts rem. Work even until this side meas the same as the other side.

Adult small, medium, large, extra-large

Finished chest circumference: 40 (44, 48, 52)"

MATERIALS

11 (12, 13, 14) skeins Jo Sharp Wool (50 grams/ 107 yards; 100% wool)

1 pair size 4 needles, or size needed to obtain gauge

1 pair size 6 needles, or size needed to obtain gauge

2 stitch holders

Yarn needle

T-pins

GAUGE

18 stitches and 24 rows = 4 inches in stockinette stitch on larger needles

BO this group of sts. (As you have seen, because you can only BO sts at the beginning of a row, neck shaping is worked by BO sts at the beginning of RS rows for one side, and at the beginning of WS rows for the other side.)

MAKE SLEEVES

With smaller needles, CO 34 (36, 38, 40) sts. Work in St st for 3", ending after you have completed a WS row. Change to larger needles and begin increasing to shape sleeve. (If you make your increases inside the selvedge (edge) sts at each side, your work will have neater selvedges, and it will be easier to sew the seams together.) On the next RS row, knit 1, increase 1 by knitting into the front and back of the next st (see page 52), knit to last 2 sts, increase 1 by knitting into the front and back of the next st, end knit 1—36 (38, 40, 42) sts. Purl one row, knit one row, purl one row. Continue to work in this manner, increasing 1 st at each side every 4th row (increase on RS row, then work 3 rows without shaping), until you have increased 1 st at each side 22 (23, 23, 24) more times, to finish with 80 (84, 86, 90) sts. Work even (without further shaping) until piece meas 18 (18¹/2, 19, 19¹/2)". In order to measure from the bottom edge, you will need to unroll the natural curl. BO all sts. Make a second sleeve the same as the first.

SEW ONE SHOULDER SEAM

Follow the instructions for sewing one shoulder seam as for the child's pullover on page 82.

FINISH NECKLINE & SEW SECOND SHOULDER SEAM

With the RS of the work facing you and using smaller needles, beginning at the right back neck where shoulder seam ended, pick up 78 (82, 86, 90) sts around neck opening (see page 82) as follows: pick up and knit 29 (31, 33, 35) sts from back neck holder, 14 sts from left shoulder seam to front holder, 21 (23, 25, 27) stitches from holder, 14 sts from holder to end of right shoulder. Purl the next row on WS. Working back and forth in St st as established, work 4 more rows, ending after you have completed a WS row. Now decrease to make the neckline a little more snug as follows: *K6, k2tog (knit 2 together; see page 53); repeat from * 9 (10, 10, 11) times and k6 (2, 6, 2), to finish with 69 (72, 76, 79) sts. Continue working in St st until piece measures 3" from the pick-up row. BO all sts loosely but neatly. You may find it helpful to use the larger size needle for working the BO row. Sew the other shoulder and neckband seam, and if you like, reverse the seam allowance in the last 1" of the neckband so the seam will not show when the neckline edge rolls to the outside.

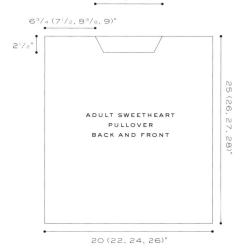

SEW IN SLEEVES

Sew in sleeves as for child's sweater (see page 83), placing removable markers or pins 9 (9¹/4, 9¹/2, 10)" from the shoulder seam along each side of the front and back.

SEW SLEEVE AND SIDE SEAMS.

Follow the instructions for sewing in the sleeves of the child's pullover on page 83, using extra pins to accommodate the larger size. Weave in ends. Block according to instructions on page 24.

HARVARD SQUARE CARDIGAN

This sweater, which combines multicolored stripes in garter and seed stitch, was inspired by a sweater Kristin saw a young girl wearing in Harvard Square. Like the Garter Stitch Cardigan (page 70) and Nordic Cardigan (page 92), it is knit in one piece to the armholes, then divided for the back, left front, and right front. Instead of cutting each yarn as you change colors in the stripe sequence, we suggest that you carry all of the colors up the side of the work by wrapping the colors not in use around the working yarn at the beginning of RS rows. To demonstrate the versatility of the knitted fabric, we had this sweater knitted twice, and assembled it in two ways: one with what is usually considered the "right" side out (see left), and the other "wrong" side out (see page 89). Teach your children this kind of flexible thinking and perhaps they will be accepted at Harvard.

SIZES

3 months, 6 months, 9 months, 12 months, 18 months, 24 months

Finished chest circumference, buttoned: 19 (21^1/4, 23, 25^1/2, 28, 30)"

Shown in sizes 9 months and 12 months

MATERIALS

1 skein Muench Wollywash (50 grams/137 yards; 100% machine-washable wool) in each of the following colors: dark purple #139; green #124; red #C40; gold #D5; and orange #E119

29-inch circular needles in size 4, or size needed to obtain gauge

29-inch circular needles in size 6, or size needed to obtain gauge

2 stitch holders

Four ^{1}/2-inch buttons

T-pins

Yarn needle

Split ring or other removable markers

GAUGE

22 sts and 44 rows = 4" in garter stitch on large needles

CHOOSE SIZE

This pattern includes six sizes. The first number given refers to size 3 months, and the numbers in parentheses refer to sizes 6 months, 9 months, 12 months, 18 months, and 24 months, in that order. To make it easier to follow the instructions, choose the size you want to make and go through the pattern and highlight all of the numbers that apply to that size. If you do not want to write directly in the book, photocopy the instructions and highlight the copy.

MAKE A GAUGE SWATCH

Using larger needles, cast on 27 stitches and work in garter stitch for approximately 5". Block the swatch the way you intend to block the finished sweater (see page 24). Measure your gauge over a 4-inch square section of the swatch. It is important that you match both the stitch gauge and row gauge.

START BODY

With smaller needle and dark purple, CO (cast on) 105 (117, 127, 141, 155, 165) sts (stitches).

Work in St st (stockinette stitch; knit 1 row, purl 1 row, repeat) for 4 rows. Then, purl one row, knit one row. Place a split ring or waste yarn marker at the end of each side of the fabric. You will refer to these markers later when picking up sts around the center front opening. Beg (begin) Harvard Square stripe sequence (see right) with row 3 for this repeat only. (For remainder of sweater, repeat rows 1 to 32.) Work until piece meas (measures) 1 1/2", unrolling to meas from cast-on edge. Change to larger needle by working the next row with the larger needle, and put aside the smaller needle until you need it again. Continue in pattern as est (established) until piece meas 5 (5 1/2, 6, 6 1/2, 7 1/2, 8 1/2)" from cast-on edge, and ending with a WS (wrong-side) row. Here is where you decide which face of the stripe pattern will be the right side of your garment. Use a waste yarn tie or a removable marker (split-ring or coil-less safety pin) to mark the right side. On the next RS (right-side) row, divide the work at

the armholes into 2 fronts and a back as follows: Work 26 (29, 32, 35, 39, 41) sts for right front, slip these stitches to a holder, work next 53 (59, 63, 71, 77, 83) sts for the back, drop the working yarn, and slip the rem (remaining) 26 (29, 32, 35, 39, 41) sts for the left front to another holder. Make a note of where you are in the stripe sequence chart, then resume working on the back sts only until the piece meas 9 1/2 (10, 11, 12, 13 1/2, 15)" from the beginning. BO (bind off) all sts.

SHAPE V-NECK AND FINISH RIGHT FRONT

Transfer the 26 (29, 32, 35, 39, 41) sts for the right front (the first stitches you put on a holder) to your knitting needle. Join a new ball of yarn at the armhole edge and continue in stripe pattern as est until piece meas 6 (6, 6 1/2, 7 1/4, 8 1/2, 9 3/4)" and you are ready to work a RS row (center

front edge of cardigan). On next row, begin shaping V-neck by BO 1 st at beginning of row, work to end—25 (28, 31, 34, 38, 40) sts rem. Work 1 row even (without shaping). Continue to BO 1 st at beginning of RS rows every other row (work 1 BO row, work 1 row even) 7 (3, 3, 2, 5, 4) more times— 18 (25, 28, 32, 33, 36) sts rem. Then BO 1 st every 4th row (work BO row, work 3 rows without shaping) 4 (8, 10, 11, 10, 11) times—14 (17, 18, 21, 23, 25) sts rem. Work even until piece meas 9 1/2 (10, 11, 12, 13 1/2, 15)" from cast-on edge. BO all shoulder sts.

FINISH LEFT FRONT

Transfer the 26 (29, 32, 35, 39, 41) sts for the left front (the sts on the last holder) to your knitting needle. Join a new ball of yarn at the armhole edge and continue in stripe pattern as established until piece meas

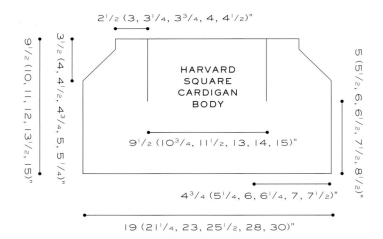

2 1/2 (3, 3 1/4, 3 3/4, 4, 4 1/2)"

9 1/2 (10, 11, 12, 13 1/2, 15)"

3 1/2 (4, 4 1/2, 4 3/4, 5, 5 1/4)"

HARVARD SQUARE CARDIGAN BODY

5 (5 1/2, 6, 6 1/2, 7 1/2, 8 1/2)"

9 1/2 (10 3/4, 11 1/2, 13, 14, 15)"

4 3/4 (5 1/4, 6, 6 1/4, 7, 7 1/2)"

19 (21 1/4, 23, 25 1/2, 28, 30)"

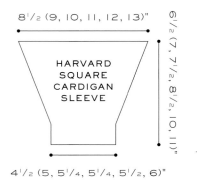

8 1/2 (9, 10, 11, 12, 13)"

HARVARD SQUARE CARDIGAN SLEEVE

6 1/2 (7, 7 1/2, 8 1/2, 10, 11)"

4 1/2 (5, 5 1/4, 5 1/4, 5 1/2, 6)"

HARVARD SQUARE
STRIPE SEQUENCE

The 32-row repeat of the stripe pattern will measure approximately 3" high.

STRIPE SEQUENCE

ROWS 1 AND 2: KNIT IN DARK PURPLE.

ROWS 3 AND 4: KNIT IN DARK GREEN.

ROWS 5 AND 6: KNIT IN RED.

ROWS 7 AND 8: KNIT IN GOLD.

ROWS 9 AND 10: KNIT IN GREEN.

ROWS 11 AND 12: KNIT IN ORANGE.

ROWS 13 AND 14: KNIT IN DARK PURPLE.

ROW 15: KNIT IN GOLD.

ROWS 16-20: WORK IN SEED STITCH IN GOLD.

For seed stitch worked over an odd number of stitches, *k1, p1, repeat from * (in other words, keep repeating k1, p1 across the row) to the last st, end k1. Work all rows the same.

For seed stitch worked over an even number of stitches, work the first row as *k1, p1, repeat from * to end. Then work the second row as *p1, k1, repeat from * to end. Repeat these 2 rows for pattern.

ROWS 21 AND 22: KNIT IN RED.

ROWS 23 AND 24: KNIT IN GREEN.

ROWS 25 AND 26: KNIT IN DARK PURPLE.

ROW 27: KNIT IN ORANGE.

ROWS 28-32: WORK IN SEED STITCH IN ORANGE AS DEFINED FOR ROWS 16–20.

Repeat these 32 rows throughout for stripe pattern.

6 (6, 6$^{1/2}$, 7$^{1/2}$, 8$^{1/2}$, 9$^{3/4}$)" and you are ready to work a WS row (center front edge of cardigan). On next row, begin shaping V-neck by BO 1 st at beginning of row, work to end—25 (28, 31, 34, 38, 40) sts rem. Work 1 row even. Continue to BO 1 st at beginning of WS rows every other row (work 1 BO row, work 1 row even) 7 (3, 3, 2, 5, 4) more times—18 (25, 28, 32, 33, 36) sts rem. Then BO 1 st every 4th row (work BO row, work 3 rows without shaping) 4 (8, 10, 11, 10, 11) times—14 (17, 18, 21, 23, 25) sts rem. Work even until piece meas 9$^{1/2}$ (10, 11, 12, 13$^{1/2}$, 15)" from cast-on edge. BO all shoulder sts. (As you have seen, because you can only BO sts at the beginning of a row, neck shaping is worked by BO sts at the beginning of RS rows for one side, and at the beginning of WS rows for the other side).

MAKE SLEEVES

With smaller needle and dark purple, CO 25 (27, 29, 29, 31, 33) sts. Work in St st for 4 rows, beginning with a knit row. Then purl 1 row, knit 1 row. Beg color stripe sequence with row 3 and work in pattern until piece meas 2" from cast-on edge. Change to larger needles, and mark the RS with a removable marker. Beginning with next RS row, increase 1 st at each edge as follows: knit into front and back of first stitch (see page 52), work to last stitch in row, knit into front and back of last stitch—27 (29, 31, 31, 33, 35) sts. Continue to increase 1 st at each side every 5th row (work an increase row, then work 4 rows without shaping) 10 (10, 12, 15, 17, 18) more times to give 47 (49, 55, 61, 67, 71) sts. When piece meas 6$^{1/2}$ (7, 7$^{1/2}$, 8$^{1/2}$, 10, 11)", BO all sts.

SEW THE SEAMS

Weave in the ends on body and sleeves of the sweater, tightening any loose edge stitches so their tension matches that of the main fabric. Using a yarn needle, sew the shoulder seams following illustration on page 23 labeled Bind Off to Bind Off. Sew the sleeve seams following the illustration labeled Rows to Rows. Sew the sleeves into the armhole opening as follows: Using T-pins, pin the sleeve seam to the bottom of the armhole (where you divided the body into fronts and back). Pin the midpoint of the top of the sleeve to the shoulder seam. Gently stretch both edges and place another pin halfway down on each side to attach each sleeve to the body. These 4 pins will give you a guideline for making the seam as smooth as possible. To sew the seam, follow the mattress stitch illustration labeled Rows to Bind Off, skipping every other row because in garter stitch there are just about twice as many rows as stitches.

Your own judgment is the best tool for making neat seams. Look at your work, and be prepared to undo and redo a section of the seam if the pieces aren't joining together smoothly. While you are sewing, be sure to pull along the length of the seam firmly to stretch out the sewn stitches so they lie flat. If the stitches are too tight, they will pucker.

FRONT BAND

Using removable markers or waste yarn ties, mark the position of 4 buttonholes on the right front for a girl, or left front for a boy, the lowest buttonhole slightly above the stitch marker near the bottom edge, and the highest at the beginning of the V-neck shaping, with the others evenly spaced in between. (Alternatively, mark buttonholes on both sides in order to make the sweater unisex). With RS facing, beginning at the lowest stitch marker, using purple and smaller needle, pick up and knit 126 (136, 153, 168, 186, 202) stitches around the front opening as follows (see instructions for picking up stitches on page 75): 30 (30, 35, 39, 46, 53) sts along right front from marker to beginning of V-neck shaping, 21 (25, 28, 30, 31, 32) sts from V-neck shaping to right shoulder seam, 24 (26, 27, 30, 32, 32) sts across back neck from shoulder seam to shoulder seam, 21 (25, 28, 30, 31, 32) sts from left shoulder seam to V-neck shaping, 30 (30, 35, 39, 46, 53) sts from V-neck shaping to marker at lower left front. Knit 1 row on WS. You will work a simple 1-row buttonhole at each of these marked positions on the next row. To make buttonhole, knit to marker, yo, k2tog (see page 53). On the next row, work yo as a knit stitch. Knit 2 more rows. BO on next RS row in knit stitch. Sew on buttons to correspond to buttonholes. If you made buttonholes on both sides of the garment, sew buttons on top of the unused buttonholes on the appropriate side for the first child who will wear it. Let lower edges roll at bottom of cardigan and sleeves. Block as instructed on page 24.

BABY SIZING TIPS

Babies are born and grow at very different rates, which can make it difficult to choose a size for a baby you don't see often. Consider the following tips:

• *If you are knitting for an unborn child, find out when the baby is due and make sure you knit a garment that is likely to fit during the appropriate season.*

• *If the baby has already been born, ask the parents to measure a sweater or sweatshirt the baby already has and tell you how well that garment fits. Remember that sweaters designed to be worn over other clothing need to be roomier than garments that are worn directly against the skin. Match the chest measurement the parent gives you to the closest chest measurement in the pattern. If the measurements don't match exactly, go up a size in the pattern.*

• *Ask the parents what size the child wears in a particular store's brand of baby clothing, then go to that store and measure their garments. Some companies print sizing charts for their clothing and distribute them at their stores and on their websites, which makes this task even easier. Again, when in doubt, go up a size.*

• *Consider making a sweater in a larger size than the baby will wear when you present the sweater so that the baby can wear it over a long period of time—in the beginning, the sweater will be oversized, generally an adorable look. To demonstrate our point, on page 134 we show the same 12-month-size Aran Pullover on a baby and a toddler.*

• *Plan a size that will fit the baby during the first sweater season after you finish knitting the sweater or later, not the size that fits the baby when you start, or the size that will fit the baby in a summer month (if that's when you think you'll finish knitting).*

NORDIC CARDIGAN

SIZES

3 months, 6 months, 9 months,
12 months, 18 months, 24 months

Finished chest circumference,
buttoned: 19¹/4 (21¹/4, 23¹/4, 25,
28, 30)"

Shown in size 9 months

MATERIALS

Muench Wollywash (50 grams/
137 yards; 100% machine-washable
wool)

4 (4, 4, 4, 5, 5) skeins in
slate blue #104

1 (1, 2, 2, 2, 2) skeins in
natural #26

29-inch circular needle in size 5,
or size needed to obtain gauge

20-inch circular needle in size 6,
or size needed to obtain gauge

Five ¹/2-inch buttons

2 stitch holders

T-pins

Yarn needle

Split ring or other
removable markers

GAUGE

25 stitches and 30 rows = 4"
in stranded colorwork patterns
on larger needles

24 sts and 28 rows = 4"
in stockinette stitch in single color
on larger needles

This simplified, modern interpretation of a traditional Scandinavian sweater style is knitted in one piece to the armholes, then divided at the armholes into the fronts and back. The body of the sweater is worked in a repeating diamond motif. The sleeves are worked with a small dot (often called lice) motif. Both motifs are shown in charts on page 96.

CHOOSE SIZE

This pattern includes six sizes. The first number given refers to size 3 months, and the numbers in parentheses refer to sizes 6 months, 9 months, 12 months, 18 months, and 24 months, in that order. To make it easier to follow the instructions, choose the size you want to make and go through the pattern and highlight all of the numbers that apply to that size. If you do not want to write directly in the book, photocopy the instructions and highlight the copy.

MAKE A GAUGE SWATCH

Using larger needles, cast on approximately 30 stitches and work in St st (stockinette stitch; knit 1 row, purl 1 row, repeat) for approximately 5". Block the swatch the way you intend to block the finished sweater (see page 24). Measure your gauge over a 4-inch square section of the swatch. It is important that you match both the stitch gauge and row gauge.

START BODY

With smaller needles and blue yarn, CO (cast on) 111 (123, 135, 147, 165, 177) sts (stitches). Work back and forth in St st for 1¹/2", ending with a WS (wrong-side) row. Change to larger needles by working the next row with the larger needles. Set aside the smaller needles for now. Work in St st until piece meas (measures) 2¹/2", ending with a RS (right-side) row. On the next WS row, purl across, inc (increasing) 10 sts evenly as follows: p11 (14, 17, 20, 20, 23), knit into front and back of next st (see page 52), *p10 (11, 12, 13, 15, 16), knit into front and back of next stitch; repeat from * 9 times (which means repeat the section following the * over and over until the end of the row, 9 times in

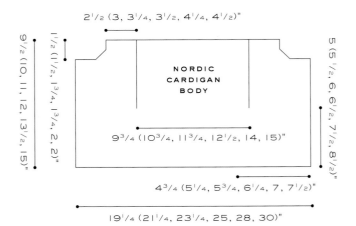

2½ (3, 3¼, 3½, 4¼, 4½)"

9½ (10, 11, 12, 13½, 15)"

1½ (1½, 1¾, 1¾, 2, 2)"

NORDIC CARDIGAN BODY

5 (5½, 6, 6½, 7½, 8½)"

9¾ (10¾, 11¾, 12½, 14, 15)"

4¾ (5¼, 5¾, 6¼, 7, 7½)"

19¼ (21¼, 23¼, 25, 28, 30)"

9 (9, 10, 11, 12, 13)"

NORDIC CARDIGAN SLEEVE

6½ (7, 7½, 8½, 10, 11)"

5 (5, 5½, 5½, 6, 6½)"

all)—121 (133, 145, 157, 175, 187) sts. Begin working in Diamond Stitch as shown on chart on page 96. Remember to strand the color not being used loosely across back of work to avoid puckering the pattern (see page 69). Most beginners tend to pull too tightly, rather than work too loosely. To avoid this, when changing colors, get into the habit of spreading out the stitches on the right needle before you work the first stitch in the new color.

DIVIDE FOR ARMHOLES

Work in pattern as est (established) until the piece meas 5 (5½, 6, 6½, 7½, 8½)" from beginning, ending having just completed a WS row. On the next row, divide the work at the armholes into two fronts and

a back as follows: Work 30 (33, 36, 39, 44, 47) sts for right front, slip these sts to a holder, work next 61 (67, 73, 79, 87, 93) sts for the back, drop the working yarn, and slip the 30 (33, 36, 39, 44, 47) sts for the left front to another holder. Resume working on the back sts only until the piece meas 9½ (10, 11, 12, 13½, 15)" from the beginning. BO (bind off) all sts.

FINISH RIGHT FRONT

Transfer the 30 (33, 36, 39, 44, 47) sts for the right front (the first stitches you put on a holder) to your knitting needle. Join a new ball of yarn at the armhole edge and resume working in est Diamond Stitch pattern, until piece meas 8 (8½, 9¼, 10¼, 11½, 13)", ending having just completed a

WS row. On next row, to begin shaping the neckline, bind off 10 (10, 11, 12, 13, 15) sts at beginning of row, then work to the end of the row. Turn and work the rem (remaining) 20 (23, 25, 27, 31, 32) sts. Turn work. You are now at center front edge of work again. Decrease 1 st by knitting first 2 sts together (see page 53), then work to end of row—19 (22, 24, 26, 30, 31) sts. Work the next WS row even (without any shaping). Decrease 1 st at beginning of every RS row 3 more times (work 1 decrease row, work 1 row even, repeat 3 times). When you finish your decreases, you will have 16 (19, 21, 23, 27, 28) sts on your needles. Work even on these sts until the right front meas the same as the back—9½ (10, 11, 12, 13½, 15)". BO all sts.

FINISH LEFT FRONT

Transfer the 30 (33, 36, 39, 44, 47) sts for the left front (the sts still on a holder) to your knitting needle. Join a new ball of yarn at the armhole edge and resume working in est Diamond Stitch pattern, until piece meas 8 (8$^{1}/_2$, 9$^{1}/_4$, 10$^{1}/_4$, 11$^{1}/_2$, 13)", ending having just completed a RS row. On next row, to begin shaping the neckline, BO 10 (10, 11, 12, 13, 15) sts at beginning of row as if to purl, then work to the end of the row. Turn and work back across the rem 20 (23, 25, 27, 31, 32) sts. Turn work. You are now at center front edge of work again. Decrease 1 st by purling the first 2 sts together, then work to end of row—19 (22, 24, 26, 30, 31) sts. Work the next RS row even. Decrease 1 st at beginning of every WS row 3 more times (work 1 decrease row, work 1 row even, repeat 3 times). When you finish your decreases, you will have 16 (19, 21, 23, 27, 28) sts on your needles. Work even on these sts until the left front meas the same as the back—9$^{1}/_2$ (10, 11, 12, 13$^{1}/_2$, 15)". BO all sts.

MAKE SLEEVES

With smaller needles and blue yarn, CO 30 (30, 33, 33, 36, 39) sts. Work in St st for 1$^{1}/_2$", ending after having just completed a WS row. On the next RS row, change to larger needles and knit across, inc (increasing) 2 sts as follows: k10 (10, 11, 11, 12, 13), *knit into front and back of same st, k9 (9, 10, 10, 11, 12); repeat from * 2 times—32 (32, 35, 35, 38, 41) sts. Work in St st until piece meas 2$^{1}/_2$" from cast-on edge, ending after having just completed a WS row. In the next RS row, inc 3 (3, 0, 4, 5, 2) sts as follows:—k8 (8, 35, 7, 8, 13); *knit into front and back of same st, k7 (7, 0, 6, 5, 13), repeat from * 3 (3, 0, 4, 5, 2) times—35 (35, 35, 39, 43, 43) sts. Purl 1 row. Beg working in Lice Stitch pattern from chart. Shape sleeve by inc 1 st each side every other row (work 1 increase row, work 1 row even without shaping) 10 (10, 12, 12, 12, 13) times; then every 4th row 1 (1, 2, 3, 4, 6) times to give 57 (57, 63, 69, 75, 81) sts. Work even until sleeve meas 6$^{1}/_2$ (7, 7$^{1}/_2$, 8$^{1}/_2$, 10, 11)" or desired length. BO all sts. Make a second sleeve same as the first.

SEW SHOULDER AND SLEEVE SEAMS

Weave in the ends on body and sleeves of the sweater. Using a yarn needle, sew the shoulder seams following mattress-stitch illustration on page 23 labeled Bind Off to Bind Off. Sew the sleeve seams following the illustration on page 45. Sew the sleeves into the armhole opening as follows: Using T-pins, pin the sleeve seam to the bottom of the armhole (where you divided the body into fronts and back). Pin the midpoint of the top of the sleeve to the shoulder seam. Gently stretch both open edges and place another pin halfway down on each side to attach each sleeve to the body. These 4 pins will give you a guideline for making the seam as smooth as possible. Use the mattress-stitch illustration labeled Rows to Bind Off (see page 23) to join the sleeves to the body. Your own judgment is the best tool for making neat seams. Look at your work, and be prepared to undo and redo a section of the seam if the pieces aren't joining together smoothly. While you are sewing, be sure to pull along the length of the seam firmly to stretch out the sewn stitches so they lie flat. If the stitches are too tight, they will pucker.

DIAMOND AND LICE STITCHES

Below are two colorwork charts for the Nordic Cardigan. Each chart shows one repeat, plus any edge stitches needed to balance the design. Always work the charts from bottom to top. When you reach row 6, return to row 1.

DIAMOND STITCH
REPEAT OF 6 STS + 1,
AND 6 ROWS

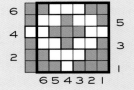

LICE STITCH
REPEAT OF 4 STS + 3,
AND 6 ROWS

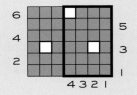

KEY

☐ IN MAIN COLOR,
KNIT ON RS OF WORK,
PURL ON WS OF WORK

☐ IN CONTRAST COLOR,
KNIT ON RS OF WORK,
PURL ON WS OF WORK

☐ PATTERN REPEAT
INDICATED BY BOX

DIAMOND STITCH
(for right front, left front, and body of cardigan)

ON RS (KNIT) ROWS: Working from right to left, work the 6-stitch repeat (from stitch 1 to stitch 6) over and over until you reach the last stitch (the one outside the heavy outline repeat box), then work that stitch— called the edge stitch (always in blue except in row 4).

ON WS (PURL) ROWS: Working from left to right, work the first stitch outside the repeat box once— called the edge stitch (always in blue except in row 4) — then work the 6-stitch repeat (from stitch 6 to stitch 1) over and over until you reach the end of the row.

LICE STITCH
(for sleeves)

ON RS (KNIT) ROWS: Working from right to left, work the 4-stitch repeat (from stitch 1 to stitch 4) over and over until you reach the last 3 stitches— called edge stitches—then work the 3 stitches outside the repeat box one time (always in blue except the second stitch from the end on row 3).

ON WS (PURL) ROWS: Working from left to right, work the first 3 stitches (the ones outside the repeat box) one time, then work the 4-stitch repeat (from stitch 4 to stitch 1) over and over until you reach the end of the row.

WORKING LICE STITCH WHILE INCREASING FOR SLEEVE: When shaping the sleeves, you will need a strategy for working the increased stitches into the lice stitch pattern. On the first increase row, place a marker after the first stitch (in between the 2 sts worked into the same stitch), and before the last stitch (again, between the 2 sts worked into the same stitch). The stitches between the markers are your original stitches; the stitches outside the markers are your new increased stitches. Work the stitches outside the markers in the background color until enough stitches have been increased to make a whole new repeat. In the case of the lice pattern, this will be 4 stitches outside the markers at each side. On the next row, you can remove the markers, and work across all stitches in pattern. When it is time to increase again, mark off the new stitches at each side as above, and work them in background color until there are enough for another full repeat at each side, then proceed as before.

MEMORIZING COLORWORK

There are many techniques for memorizing repeats in stranded colorwork so that eventually you can work without constantly referring to the chart, such as finding the "rhythm" of the pattern repeat, or determining the logical color sequence of the row you are working by comparing it to the previous row.

FINDING THE "RHYTHM"

Following the Diamond Stitch chart, from right to left for rows 3 and 5 (both the same), the rhythm is 1, 2, 1, 2, 1, 2, etc., which translates to 1 blue, 2 white, 1 blue, 2 white, etc.

FINDING THE LOGICAL SEQUENCE

If you compare rows 1 and 2 of the Diamond Stitch chart, you will see that in row 2, three centered white stitches are worked above each single white stitch in row 1. So, when working row 2, you know every time you approach a white stitch, you work 1 white stitch before the existing white stitch, 1 white stitch into the existing white stitch, and 1 white stitch after the existing white stitch.

MAKE NECKBAND

Using smaller needles and blue yarn, with RS facing and beginning at right front neck shaping, pick up and knit 68 (68, 76, 80, 84, 92) sts around neck opening as follows (refer to illustration on page 82, if necessary): 19 (19, 22, 23, 24, 27) sts from center front edge to right shoulder seam, 30 (30, 32, 34, 36, 38) sts across back neck to left shoulder seam, 19 (19, 22, 23, 24, 27) sts from left shoulder seam to beginning of left front neck shaping. Work in 2x2 rib (knit 2, purl 2, repeat to end of row) for 5 rows, and end having just completed a WS row. Using larger needles, BO all sts in rib pattern.

MAKE BUTTON BAND

Traditionally, boys have their buttonholes on the left front, and girls have their buttonholes on the right front. If you prefer, you can make buttonholes on both fronts by skipping the button band and working both sides as buttonhole bands (see right). (If you are making buttonholes on both sides, when you have decided which side will have the buttons, sew the buttons on top of the unused buttonholes).

To make button band, using smaller needles and blue yarn, with RS facing and beginning at the lower edge for right front, or neck edge for left front, pick up and knit 48

(52, 56, 60, 68, 76) sts evenly along front opening of garment, beginning or ending $^{3}/_{4}$" from bottom of sweater (this gives the bottom a chance to roll up). Work in 2x2 rib as for neckband for 5 rows. BO all sts loosely and evenly in rib pattern.

BUTTONHOLE BAND

Mark the positions for 5 buttonholes, the lowest $^{3}/_{4}$" up from the bottom edge, the highest centered on the neckband, and the other 3 evenly spaced in between. Using smaller needles and blue yarn, with RS facing, pick up and knit 48 (52, 56, 60, 68, 76) sts as for button band. Work 2 rows in 2x2 rib. On next row work in 2x2 rib to marked buttonhole position, *yo (make a yarnover; see page 53), k2tog, work to next marked position; repeat from * until all buttonholes are finished, then work in 2x2 rib as est to end. Work 2 more rows 2x2 rib. BO all sts loosely and evenly in rib pattern.

FINISHING

Sew on 5 buttons. Let edges roll to outside at bottom of body and sleeves. Weave in loose ends. Block according to instructions on page 24.

AN ESPECIALLY CONVENIENT—AND LOGICAL—WAY TO KNIT TUBULAR SHAPES,
SUCH AS THE BODIES AND SLEEVES OF SWEATERS, MITTENS, GLOVES, AND HATS,
IS TO KNIT THEM IN THE ROUND ON CIRCULAR OR DOUBLE-POINTED NEEDLES.
WHEN YOU DO THIS YOU HAVE VERY FEW SEAMS TO SEW TOGETHER AFTER THE
KNITTING IS COMPLETE AND THE RIGHT SIDE OF THE WORK IS ALWAYS FACING
OUT, WHICH MEANS IF YOU ARE WORKING IN STOCKINETTE STITCH YOU NEVER
HAVE TO PURL. IT ALSO SIMPLIFIES STRANDED COLORWORK BECAUSE IT
ALLOWS YOU TO LOOK AT THE RIGHT SIDE OF YOUR WORK THROUGHOUT, THE
WAY IT APPEARS IN THE CHARTS.

CIRCULAR KNITTING

chapter 6

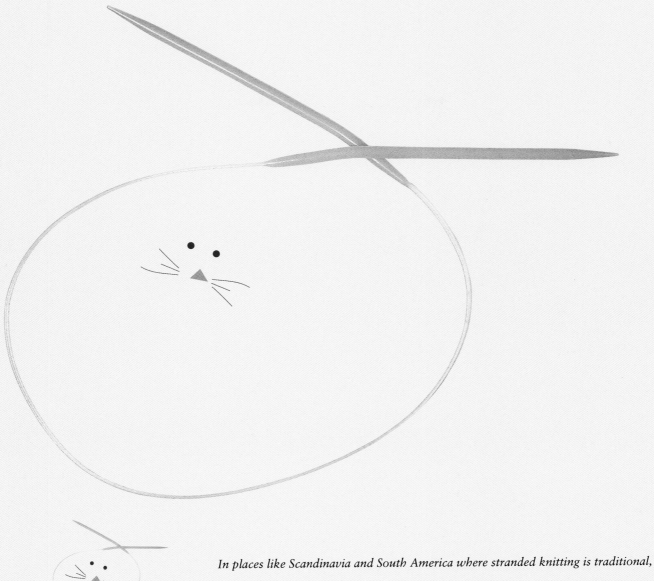

In places like Scandinavia and South America where stranded knitting is traditional, knitting in the round is prevalent. In other parts of the world, you're likely to find devotees of both knitting in the round and knitting back and forth in flat pieces, some with very strong opinions about which technique is "better." We suggest that you remain open to the possibilities of both, try to learn both methods well, then pick and choose the one that appeals to you and makes the most sense on a project-by-project basis.

KNITTING IN THE ROUND

The crucial point when you are starting to knit in the round, is at the end of the first round when you join the first and last cast-on stitches. You must keep the cast-on edge at the inside of the circle; if you don't you will introduce a twist into the work, which can only be fixed by ripping out and starting over. If you are having trouble joining the first and last cast-on stitches to start the first round, consider knitting the first couple of inches of your project back and forth, then joining the first and last stitches when you have some knitted fabric to grasp, and you can very easily see whether or not the fabric is twisted. When the project is finished, you will need to sew together the open seam where you started.

ON CIRCULAR NEEDLES

Circular knitting needles look like two short straight needles connected in the center with a flexible coated wire or cable. To knit with them in the round, you cast on as usual, then join the first and last stitches to each other to close the circle. To accommodate different project sizes, circular needles are sold in a variety of lengths. If you try to use circular needles that are too long for a project, they will not work because you will not be able to join the first and last cast-on stitches. If you try to knit with circular needles that are too short, you will not have enough room on your needles for all of the stitches. Fortunately, if you are knitting with the incorrect length needle, you will know right away when you try to join, or when you run out of room when casting on.

1) To begin a project to be knit in the round, cast on the desired number of stitches on one end of the circular needle as usual (as you would if you were using a straight needle). Spread all the stitches out so they cover the first needle, the wire, and the second needle. Lay your work down on a flat surface in a circular shape with the cast-on edge on the inside of the circle, the first cast-on stitch at the left, and the last cast-on stitch (the one with the working yarn attached) at the right. Make sure the cast-on stitches run straight around the inside of the circle without spiraling around the needles or the connecting cable. Untwist the cast-on row, if necessary. Place a marker on the end of the right needle. This marker will remind you as you are knitting that you are finishing one round and beginning another round.

2) Raise your needles (the right needle in your right hand, the left needle in your left hand, the wire hanging down between them, and the cast-on edge at the inside of the circle). Insert the right-hand needle into the first stitch on the left-hand needle (the first cast-on stitch) and knit it as usual, making sure that the marker doesn't escape as you work the first stitch. Be sure to pull firmly on the working yarn after the first stitch so that the first and last cast-on stitches are snuggled up tightly against each other (you do not want a gap here). Knit all of the stitches until you come to the marker. You are now at the end of the first round. Slip the marker to your right-hand needle. You are now at the beginning of the second round. Continue knitting around and around as required for your project.

ON DOUBLE-POINTED NEEDLES

It is possible to knit in the round on 4 or 5 double-pointed needles. This means that the stitches are divided among 3 or 4 needles and the remaining empty needle is used to work the stitches. The number of needles is usually determined by the type of project, the size of the project, and the knitter's preference. When you knit in the round on 4 double-pointed needles (stitches divided among 3 needles, with one working needle) your knitted "tube" will look like a triangle as you work. When you knit in the round on 5 double-pointed needles (stitches divided among 4 needles, with 1 working needle) your knitted "tube" will look like a square. Double-pointed needles come in a variety of lengths. It is generally most comfortable to do small projects like baby hats on relatively short needles (approximately 8" long) and larger projects, such as adult hats, on longer needles. Choose the length of the needle according to the amount of space the stitches will occupy, with about an inch or so of needle sticking out each end of your work. If the needles are too short, the stitches can easily fall off the ends of the needles, not a pleasant experience.

1) To begin knitting on double-pointed needles, cast on all of your stitches on 1 needle, then divide them among 3 or 4 needles, depending on whether you have 4 or 5 needles in all. Lay the needles down on a flat surface in either a triangle shape or a square shape (as required by the number of needles you are using), with the first and last cast-on stitches meeting at one corner, the first cast-on stitch on the left, and the last cast-on stitch (with the working yarn attached) on the right. Just as with the circular needles, make sure the cast-on stitches run straight around the inside of the shape without spiraling around any of the needles. Untwist the cast-on row, if necessary.

2) Raise all of the needles holding stitches with both hands, then transfer the needle with the first stitch cast-on to your left hand. Begin knitting the first cast-on stitch with the remaining empty needle, using the working yarn attached to the last cast-on stitch. Pull the working yarn firmly after the first stitch to close the gap at the point where the stitches from the first and last needles meet.

3) Knit to the end of the first needle. With the new empty needle, knit the stitches on the second needle. Continue until you have knitted all but 1 stitch on the last needle. Place a marker, then knit the last stitch. The marker will alert you to the fact that after you knit 1

more stitch you will have finished a round. It cannot be placed at the true end of the round because it would fall off the end of the needle. Continue knitting around and around as required for your project.

Knitting with double-pointed needles, with needles poking out at different directions, can feel a bit awkward at the start. Try to focus on the 2 working needles, and let the others hang out of the way. Once you have knitted a few rounds the growing fabric holds the needles in their correct positions and it becomes much more comfortable.

SIZES

Hat: 15 (16¹/₂, 18)" circumference, to fit 3 to 6 months (6 to 12 months, 12 to 24 months)

Shown in size 6 to 12 months

Mittens: Newborn to 6 months

MATERIALS

2 skeins Manos del Uruguay Handspun Pure Wool (100 grams/ 135 yards; 100% wool), to make hat and mittens

Shown in pink #0 and gold #Z

1 pair size 9 straight needles, or size needed to obtain gauge

1 set of 4 size 9 double-pointed needles, or size needed to obtain gauge

Stitch marker

Yarn needle

Cotton-covered elastic in matching color, to keep mittens on (optional)

GAUGE

17 sts and 24 rows = 4" on size 9 needles in stockinette stitch in the round

EARFLAP HAT AND THUMBLESS MITTENS

This warm hat can be tied at the chin or at the crown, depending on the weather and the baby's willingness to keep the hat on (if the baby tends to swat the hat off, the chin tie is the way to go). The mittens are more likely to stay on if a piece of elastic yarn is run through the wrong side of the stitches at the wrist. We used a soft handspun, kettle-dyed yarn from Uruguay for this project (as well as the Nordic Snowflake Pullover on page 106). Part of the charm of this yarn, hand-dyed by a cooperative of rural women artisans, is the subtle variation in thickness and color that occurs within each skein. Because this project is so small, it doesn't make sense to make a gauge swatch. Instead, start knitting the hat. Take your gauge when you have a few inches to measure and determine if you want to continue or start over with another size needle.

HAT

CHOOSE SIZE

This pattern includes three sizes. The first number given refers to size 3 to 6 months, and the numbers in parentheses refer to sizes 6 to 12 months, and 12 to 24 months, in that order. To make it easier to follow the instructions, choose the size you want to make and go through the pattern and highlight all of the numbers that apply to that size. If you do not want to write directly in the book, photocopy the instructions and highlight the copy.

MAKE TIES AND EARFLAPS

Using straight needles, CO (cast on) 3 sts (stitches). Work in garter stitch (knit all rows) until piece meas (measures) 12" to make the first tie. Leave sts on the needle.

Begin shaping for the ear flap by working the sts at the end of the tie as follows:
ROW 1: K1, inc 1, k1, inc 1, k1—5 sts. In other words, knit 1 stitch, increase 1 stitch using simple cast-on method (see page 52), knit 1 stitch,

increase 1 st using simple cast-on method, knit 1 stitch. When you finish the row you will have 5 sts.

ROW 2: Knit 5 sts.

ROW 3: K1, inc 1, k3, inc 1, k1—7 sts.

ROW 4: Knit all sts.

ROW 5: K1, inc 1, k5, inc 1, k1—9 sts.

ROW 6: Knit all sts.

ROW 7: K1, inc 1, k7, inc 1, k1—11 sts.

ROW 8: Knit all sts.

ROW 9: K1, inc 1, k9, inc 1, k1—13 sts.

ROW 10: Knit all sts. If you are making the smallest size, the ear flap shaping is done. For the two largest sizes, work row 11.

ROW 11: K1, inc 1, k11, inc 1, k1—15 sts.

For all sizes, continue working in garter st on 13 (15, 15) sts until flap meas 2 1/2" long from the beginning of the flap shaping (not counting the tie). BO (bind off) all sts.

Make a second tie and flap just like the first.

MAKE BODY OF HAT

Using a set of double-pointed needles, CO 63 (70, 77) sts. Place a marker before the last CO stitch, and join sts for working in the round. Work 3 garter ridges as follows:

ROUND 1: Purl

ROUND 2: Knit

ROUND 3: Purl

ROUND 4: Knit

ROUND 5: Purl (5 rounds completed to form 3 garter ridges).

Work in St st (stockinette stitch) in the round (knit all sts every round) until piece meas 3 1/4 (3 3/4, 4 1/4)".

DECREASE ROUNDS: You will make decreases in every other round. As the number of stitches gets smaller, it may be necessary to rearrange stitches on the needles by slipping them from one needle to another in order to keep approximately one-third of the stitches on each needle.

DECREASE ROUND 1: *K7 (8, 9), k2tog (knit 2 together; see page 53); rep from * around—56 (63, 70) sts. (The asterisk is used to indicate the beginning of a set of repeated instructions. In other words, you work k7 (8, 9), k2tog, k7 (8, 9), k2tog, over and over until you get to the end of the round.)

Knit next round plain.

DECREASE ROUND 2: *K6 (7, 8), k2tog; rep from * around—49 (56, 63) sts.

Knit next round plain.

DECREASE ROUND 3: *K5 (6, 7), k2tog; rep from * around—42 (49, 56) sts.

Knit next round plain.

DECREASE ROUND 4: *K4 (5, 6), k2tog; rep from * around—35 (42, 49) sts.

Knit next round plain.

DECREASE ROUND 5: *K3 (4, 5), k2tog; rep from * around—28 (35, 42) sts.

Knit next round plain.

DECREASE ROUND 6: *K2 (3, 4), k2tog; rep from * around—21 (28, 35) sts.

Knit next round plain.

DECREASE ROUND 7: *K1 (2, 3), k2tog; rep from * around—14 (21, 28) sts.

Knit next round plain.

DECREASE ROUND 8: *K0 (1, 2),

k2tog; rep from * around—7 (14, 21) sts. (When you see a direction like "K0" for your size, it means that for your particular size there is nothing to work, so you should proceed to the next instruction.)

Knit next round plain. You are now finished decreasing for the smallest size. For the two largest sizes, work additional decrease rounds as follows:

DECREASE ROUND 9: *K0 (1), k2tog; rep from * around—7 (14) sts. Knit next round plain. You are now finished decreasing for the medium size. For the largest size, continue as follows:

DECREASE ROUND 10: K2tog around—7 sts.

For all sizes, pull yarn through rem (remaining) 7 sts like a drawstring and pull tight to close top of hat.

SEW ON FLAPS

Fold the hat flat. Place a pin or marker at each fold to mark the center front and back of the hat. Pin the flaps to the cast-on edge of the hat so that the edges of the flaps are 5$^{1}/_{2}$ (5$^{3}/_{4}$, 6$^{1}/_{2}$)" apart at the front and 3$^{1}/_{2}$ (3$^{3}/_{4}$, 4$^{1}/_{2}$)" apart at the back, to allow a little extra room for baby's face. Attach the flaps to the hat using a yarn needle; although you are actually sewing the bound off edges of the flaps to the cast-on edge of the hat, follow the instructions on page 23 for sewing Bind Off to Bind Off.

MITTENS

START CUFF

CO 16 sts very loosely on a double-pointed needle. Divide the stitches among 3 double-pointed needles with 5 sts on the first and second needles, and 6 sts on the third needle; place a marker between the fifth and sixth stitch on the third needle to mark the end of the round. Beg (begin) working in the round with the fourth needle as follows: *knit 1 round, purl 1 round; repeat from * once more (4 rounds completed); work 1 more purl round (5 rounds completed to form 3 garter ridges).

ROUND 6: Increase 4 sts around as follows, *k1, inc 1 in next st, k2; rep from * 3 more times—20 sts. (In other words, knit 1 st, increase 1 by knitting into the front and back of the next st (see page 52), knit 2 sts; repeat this sequence 3 more times to finish with 20 sts).

Work in St st (stockinette stitch) in the round (knit all sts every round) until piece meas 3" from beg (beginning).

SHAPE MITTEN TOP

As the number of stitches gets smaller, it may be necessary to rearrange stitches on the needles by slipping them from one needle to another in order to keep approximately one-third of the stitches on each needle; be careful not to lose the stitch marker for the end of the round.

DECREASE ROUND 1: *K3, k2tog (knit 2 together; see page 53); rep from * 3 more times—16 sts.

Knit next round plain.

DECREASE ROUND 2: *K2, k2tog; rep from * 3 more times—12 sts.

Knit next round plain.

DECREASE ROUND 3: *K1, k2tog; rep from * 3 more times—8 sts.

Knit next round plain.

DECREASE ROUND 4: K2tog 4 times—4 sts.

Pull yarn through rem (remaining) sts like a drawstring to close the tip. Work a second mitten same as the first.

INSERT WRIST ELASTIC

To help the mitten stay on, run cotton-covered elastic around the cuff of the mitten on the wrong side of the work. If you examine the wrong side of the cuff you will see that it has 2 garter ridges, and each garter ridge is composed of alternating "smile" and "frown" loops. Thread about 12" of elastic on a yarn needle and run it through every other frown loop in the lower garter ridge. Pull the ends so there is slight tension on the elastic and tie a knot. Trim the ends to 2" long and weave them in on the wrong side. Add a second row of elastic, working through every other smile loop of the upper garter ridge and fasten off as before.

Sweaters knitted in the round with patterned yokes are a Scandinavian tradition. Although our yarn choice is nontraditional—kettle-dyed, handspun yarn from Uruguay—our construction method is standard. The body is worked in the round on circular needles, and the sleeves are worked in the round on four double-pointed needles. Then the body and sleeves are joined at the yoke on a circular needle, and the sweater is finished in one piece.

SIZES

26½" chest circumference, to fit size 12 months to 24 months. Because of the large number of stitches in the snowflake motif, this pattern cannot be easily adapted to fit a wide range of stitch counts, so it is only given in one size.

MATERIALS

Manos del Uruguay Handspun Pure Wool (100 grams/135 yards; 100% wool)

3 skeins light purple #62

1 skein light gray #22

24" circular needles in sizes 7, 8, and 9 for the body, or size needed to obtain gauge

1 set of 4 size 7 double-pointed needles, for the cast-on and first 1½" of the sleeves, or size needed to obtain gauge (same as body cast-on)

1 set of 4 size 8 double-pointed needles for the main section of the sleeves, or size needed to obtain gauge (same as used for body in one-color stockinette stitch)

Stitch markers

Yarn needle

GAUGE

17 stitches and 20 rows = 4" in two-color stranded knitting on largest needles in the round

17 stitches and 20 rows = 4" in one-color stockinette stitch on middle-size needles in the round

MAKE A GAUGE SWATCH

In order to be sure that the sweater will turn out the intended size, you need to take your gauge in the round. We suggest that you start with a sleeve, work for about 5½ inches so you have at least 4 inches of fabric worked using the middle-size needles, then check your stockinette-stitch gauge over the main section of the sleeve. You may find it easier to measure if you temporarily slip your stitches off the needles onto a smooth string so you can measure your work flat. If you have more stitches and rows to the inch than the pattern gauge, your work is too tight, and you should go up a needle size. If you have fewer stitches and rows than the pattern gauge, your work is too loose, and you should go down a needle size. Because the number of rows in the yoke is fixed, it is important that you match both the stitch gauge and row gauge for this project.

If the row gauge is off, the depth of the yoke will change, which may create problems with the fit of the upper body and shoulder area.

BEGIN BODY

With smallest circular needle and purple yarn, CO (cast on) 100 sts (stitches), place marker, and join for working in the round, taking care not to twist the cast-on sts. Work in St st (stockinette stitch; knit all rounds) for 2". Change to middle-size needles. Inc (increase) 14 sts evenly in the next round as follows: *K6, inc 1 in next st (knit into front and back of next st; see page 52); rep from * 11 more times (16 sts remaining before the marker), **k7, inc 1 in next st; repeat from ** 1 more time—114 sts. The marker indicates the place where one side seam would be if this project had seams. Place another marker bet (between) the 57th and 58th sts to

CHANGING COLORS FOR SNOWFLAKE MOTIF AT YOKE

When changing colors for the snowflake motif at the yoke, it is very important that you carry the unused color loosely across the back so the yoke will not pucker and lose elasticity. When it's time to change colors, spread out the stitches on the right-hand needle as far as they will stretch (with bigger gaps between them than they would ordinarily have); that way when you pick up the new color and carry it across the back of the spread-out stitches, you have some built-in insurance against working too tightly. Although it may seem like there is too much yarn floating behind the work, this is what you need to do to produce a flat, even fabric and to assure that the sweater will fit comfortably (if you put a baby in an uncomfortable sweater you are asking for trouble). If after working a few rounds you can see that the yoke is puckering and does not lie as flat as your one-color fabric, rip it out and start over. In the short run, you may feel frustrated. In the long run, it will be worth it—guaranteed—and you will have avoided a common beginner's pitfall.

mark the other side. Work in St st until piece meas (measures) 9" from the cast-on. On next round, BO (bind off) the first 4 sts, work to 4 sts before the second marker, BO next 8 sts, work to last 4 sts in the round (removing marker), BO 4 sts. You now have two sections of 49 sts each on the needle for the front and back. Set aside the body for now.

MAKE SLEEVES

Using smaller sleeve dpn (double-pointed needles), CO 28 sts. Divide sts evenly onto 3 needles with 9 sts on the first and second needles, and 10 sts on the third needle. Place a marker one stitch in from end of last stitch on last needle, join for working in the round, and work in St st for 1¹/2". Change to larger sleeve dpn. Inc 6 sts evenly in the next round as follows: *K4, inc 1 in next st (knit into front and back of next st); rep from * 3 more times (8 sts remaining unworked), **k3, inc 1 in next st; rep from ** 1 more time—34 sts. Place another marker

between the first and second sts in the round. The 2 sts between the markers indicate where the seam line would be, if this project had seams, and will indicate where the sleeve shaping goes. Beginning with the next round, shape sleeve as follows:

INCREASE ROUND: K1, sl (slip) marker, inc 1 in next st (knit into front and back of next stitch), knit to 1 st before the next marker, inc 1 in next st, sl marker, k1—36 sts.

Knit 3 rounds without shaping.

Repeat the last 4 rounds (an increase round followed by 3 rounds without shaping) 6 more times—48 sts. Work one more increase round—50 sts. Work even (without further shaping) until sleeve meas 10" from cast-on edge. On the next row, BO the first 4 sts, work to last 4 sts, BO 4 sts. You now have 42 sts on needles for main sleeve section. Place the 42 main sleeve sts on a string or large stitch holder and set aside. Make a second sleeve same as the first.

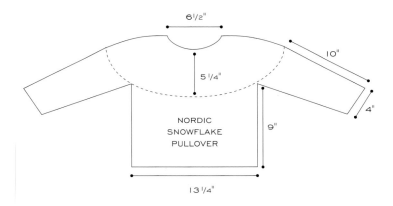

6¹/2"

10"

5¹/4"

4"

NORDIC
SNOWFLAKE
PULLOVER

9"

13¹/4"

ATTACH BODY AND SLEEVES

With largest circular needle and purple yarn, knit the first 49-st body section for the back, knit 42 sts from one sleeve, knit the other 49-st body section for front, knit 42 sts from other sleeve—182 sts on largest circular needle. Place a marker after the last st to indicate the end of the round.

This diagram shows how the stitches will be arranged on the needle, as seen from a bird's-eye view, after you have attached the body and sleeves, with the needle tip at the center of the back.

WORK TWO-COLOR YOKE FROM CHART

Work the 26 stitches of Row 1 from the snowflake chart (at right) 7 times around. Continue in pattern from chart, decreasing where indicated by either ssk or k2tog (slip, slip, knit or knit 2 together, see page 53).

Decreases are worked in the following charted rounds:

ROUND 2: Decrease 2 sts in each repeat—168 sts, 24 sts in each repeat.

ROUND 10: Decrease 2 sts in each repeat—154 sts, 22 sts in each repeat.

ROUND 25: Decrease 2 sts in each repeat—140 sts, 20 sts in each repeat.

ROUND 26: Decrease 2 sts in each repeat—126 sts, 18 sts in each repeat.

ROUND 27: Decrease 2 sts in each repeat—112 sts, 16 sts in each repeat.

In rounds 12 to 15 of the yoke pattern there are long intervals where the purple yarn is not used. In these areas, secure the unused yarn to the back of the fabric every 3–5 sts by twisting it around the working yarn. Remember to spread out the sts on the needle before you twist the yarns to avoid puckering. When round 28 has been completed, break off the purple yarn, remove any repeat markers, and work round 29 with gray only—112 sts remaining.

FINISH NECKLINE AND UNDERARM

In the next round, work ssk 56 times around—56 sts remaining. Change to smallest dpn and work in 2x2 rib (knit 2, purl 2, repeat) for 7 rounds. Change to the medium-sized needles and work 4 rounds of St st. BO very loosely as if to knit; you may find it helpful to use the largest size needle for the BO row.

Sew underarm seams together using Bind Off to Bind Off seam on page 23. Allow bottom edges to roll gently to the outside. Weave in loose ends. Block according to the instructions on page 24.

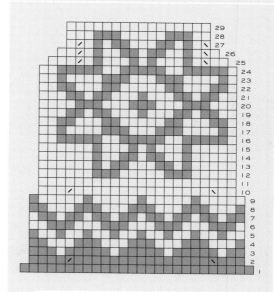

SNOWFLAKE YOKE

KEY

- ☐ KNIT WITH GRAY
- ■ KNIT WITH PURPLE
- ☑ K2TOG WITH GRAY
- ◨ SSK WITH GRAY
- ◪ K2TOG WITH PURPLE
- ◩ SSK WITH PURPLE

TIPS FOR WORKING WITH THE CHART

When you are working from a chart in the round all rows are read from right to left. To begin this chart, on the first round, work the 26-stitch repeat 7 times (easy because all the stitches are purple). On the second round, decrease 1 stitch at the 4th and 20th stitches in each 26-stitch repeat (again, all the stitches are purple), to end with a total of 24 stitches in each repeat, or 168 stitches total. Note that row 2 of the chart shows the number of stitches remaining after the decreases are worked. On round 3, the colorwork begins. To make it easier to count stitches and maintain the pattern, place markers between each pattern repeat.

STAY-ON BABY BOOTIES

SIZES

To fit newborn to 3 months

To make larger booties, use a thicker yarn (up to DK weight) and larger needles.

MATERIALS

1 skein Koigu Premium Merino Solids (50 grams/176 yards; 100% wool). Note: One skein will make 2 pairs of booties. Shown in the following colors: olive #2343, deep rose #2239, blue #2171, and pumpkin #2380.

1 set of 5 size 3 double-pointed needles, about 7"–8" long, or size needed to obtain gauge

GAUGE

6 to 6½ stitches = 1 inch in garter stitch on size 3 needles in the round

We don't know how long people have been making these booties but it must be a very long time. Years ago a 95-year-old woman sent a pattern similar to this one to the letters-to-the-editor section of Threads *magazine in hopes that publishing it would keep the design from disappearing forever. Kristin's friend Ulla, who was born in Germany, learned how to make booties like these from her mother and has been knitting them for years. When Melanie and Kristin were pregnant (coincidentally, at the same time), their friend Therese made them multiple pairs in different colors and several sizes. Aside from looking perfectly adorable, these booties stay on baby's feet better than any others we've found because of their unique shape and the tie closure.*

We recommend that you wait to try this pattern until you are feeling very comfortable with double-pointed needles. Even then, we have to admit that you might find making your first bootie a bit tricky, though, of course, we've tried to spell out the techniques very clearly to minimize any confusion. History teaches us that once a knitter masters these booties, they are likely to become a favorite project. Because this project is so small, it doesn't make sense to do a gauge swatch. Instead, cast on and start knitting, then take your gauge once you've made the bootie sides. If you're off, rip out and start over, or continue if you think the bootie looks nice and will fit a baby's foot. Be sure to make the second bootie at the same gauge as the first.

MAKE SOLE

Wind a piece of masking tape or a rubber band, or use a point protector (available in knitting shops) on one end each of two dpn (double-pointed needles) in order to temporarily transform them into a set of miniature straight needles. CO (cast on) 7 sts (stitches). Work back and forth in garter stitch (knit all stitches every row) for 15 garter ridges (30 rows). Leave the work on the needle with yarn attached. Remove stoppers from the needles to turn them back into dpn.

MAKE BOOTIE SIDES

You now have a rectangle with live stitches on a dpn at one of the short sides. Working counterclockwise, pick up stitches around the rectangle (see illustration on page 75) on the 3 remaining sides as follows: With a second double-pointed needle, pick up and knit 1 st in the ditch between each garter ridge along the first long side of the rectangle—14 picked-up stitches on the second needle. With a third dpn, pick up and knit 7 sts along the short (cast-on) edge where you began. With a fourth dpn, pick up 14 sts along the remaining long side of the rectangle as you did before. You now have 42 stitches arranged in a rectangle on 4 needles.

Using a fifth dpn, work garter stitch in the round (purl 1 row, knit 1 row, repeat) for 10 garter ridges (20 rounds), placing a stitch marker after the first st of the first round (it is placed 1 st in from the actual beginning of the round so it doesn't fall off the end of the needle). Work 1 more purl round. Remember when you work garter stitch in the round you alternate knit and purl rounds (rather than knitting all rows as in flat, back-and-forth knitting).

WORK INSTEP IN GARTER RIDGES

Knit 7 sts for the short side on the first needle, then knit 14 stitches for the first long side on the second needle. Work back and forth on the 7 sts on the third needle to make the instep as follows:

ROW 1: (You are on the right side of the work) Knit the first 6 sts on the needle—1 st remains unworked. Sl (slip) the last st purlwise from your working needle to the next long-side needle (the fourth needle of the group when you were working the sides), maintaining the correct stitch mount (see page 21), and knit these 2 sts together (the st slipped from the working needle together with the first st of the fourth needle; see page 53)—7 sts on your working short-side needle. After you have k2tog (knit 2 sts together) from the long-side needle, remember to slide the sts of the long-side needle back away from the point so they don't fall off as you continue to work. Turn your work so you can work the next row on the same stitches.

ROW 2: Knit the first 6 sts on the needle, sl the last st of the working needle to the next long-side needle (the second needle when you were working the sides), k2tog as above. Turn your work.

Repeat rows 1 and 2 until there are 8 sts remaining on each of the long-side needles—30 sts, 8 on each long-side needle, 7 on each short-side needle. You have just finished a right-side row and the working yarn is at the left side of the instep when looking down on the bootie as if you were wearing it. (If your yarn is on the right of the instep looking down on the bootie, check to make sure the toe of your bootie is not inside-out, and turn it right side out if necessary.) Knit back across the 7 sts again—you are now at the right side of the instep when looking down on the bootie as if wearing it.

WORK ANKLE

You will now resume working in the round in St st (stockinette stitch); (knit every round) for the ankle.

ROUND 1: Inc 1 st at the end of instep needle by picking up and knitting 1 st from the fabric in the space between the instep needle and the next needle and placing the new st on the instep needle—31 sts, 8 on each long-side needle, 7 on the short-side needle at back of heel, and 8 on the instep needle. Work round 1 as follows: K8 (knit 8 sts) from next long-side needle, k7 from back of heel needle, k8 from other long-side needle, inc 1 at beg (beginning) of instep needle by picking up and knitting 1 st from the fabric between the previous long-side needle and the instep needle, k8 to end of instep needle—32 sts, 8 on each long-side needle, 7 on the short-side needle at back of heel, and 9 on the instep needle.

ROUND 2: As you work this round you are going to rearrange the sts so you end up with 8 sts on each needle. Sl the last st just worked from the instep needle to a new working needle. Using this working needle, k7 sts from next long-side needle—1 st remains unworked. Sl the unworked st to the heel needle. With a new working needle, k8 from heel needle (the slipped st and the 7 sts that were already on the needle). To finish the round, working as you normally would, k8 from other long-side needle, then knit the remaining 8 sts from the instep needle—32 sts, 8 sts on each needle. Place a marker between the first and second sts of the first long-side needle to indicate the beginning of the round.

ROUND 3: Knit 1 round plain.

ROUND 4: Eyelet round: *K2, yo (yarnover, see page 53), K2tog; repeat from * 8 times around. (The asterisk is used to indicate the beginning of a set of repeated instructions. In other words, you knit 2, make a yarnover, knit 2 sts together, knit 2, make a yarnover, knit 2 sts together, etc., over and over until you get to the end of the round. In this case you work the repeated instructions a total of 8 times to form 8 yarnover eyelet holes.)

Continue knitting in the round until the stockinette stitch section of the bootie meas approximately 2". BO (bind off) all sts loosely. Make a second bootie same as the first.

MAKE BOOTIE TIES

Using double-pointed needles, make two 3-stitch I-cords, each approximately 14" long for ties, following the instructions on page 64. Alternatively, choose one of the bootie tie options listed at right. Thread ties through the eyelets and tie in a bow at instep.

OPTIONS FOR BOOTIE TIE

We made all of the booties in the photograph on page 110 with I-cord ties. Here are some other options:

• *Use a pretty, washable ribbon.*

• *Cast on 100 stitches using the knit-on cast-on method (see page 15). Break yarn. Pull the working yarn out of the last stitch to undo the stitch. Pull all of the stitches off the needle.*

• *Cast on 100 stitches. Now bind off all the stitches.*

• *Single-crochet a chain of about 100 stitches. Break yarn and draw through last stitch to finish off.*

MUCH OF THE APPEAL OF KNITTED FABRIC HAS TO DO WITH ITS TEXTURE, WHICH VARIES DEPENDING ON A VARIETY OF FACTORS, INCLUDING THE FIBER CONTENT OF THE YARN, THE WAY THE YARN IS SPUN AND PROCESSED, AND THE STITCH PATTERNS USED TO CREATE THE FABRIC.

CABLES & RIBS

chapter 7

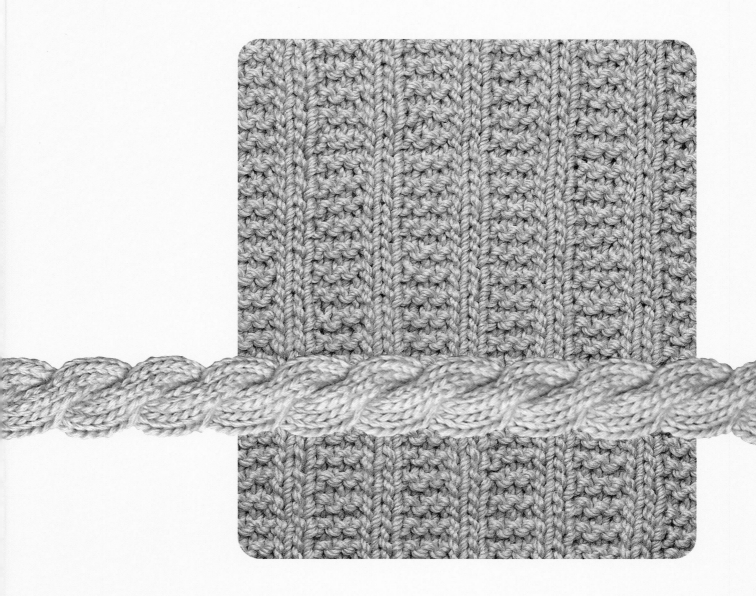

In Chapter 3, we introduced some basic stitch patterns achieved by alternating knit and purl stitches. Here, we expand on that concept by introducing cables (which are made by stitches exchanging places) and a fancy-looking rib that is actually even easier to knit than the standard "non-fancy" ribs in Chapter 3.

CABLES

Though cables appear complex, they are actually easy to produce. The only time cables become challenging is when several different kinds are used in a single project. In those cases, it is not actually the cables that present the challenge but keeping track of what is happening with each cable pattern in any given row. Markers can be tremendously helpful in these circumstances, especially at the beginning of the project before the cable pattern is memorized or the knitted fabric is far enough along to be used as a visual guide. Often, instructions for working cables are shown in chart form. In this chapter, we provide both chart and line-by-line written instructions wherever space permits because we believe that showing the pattern both ways will make the directions more clear.

WORKING MOCK CABLES

Mock cables are made without a cable needle and are generally worked on fewer stitches than true cables. Like true cables, they are made by stitches exchanging places, but in this case, the twist is achieved by simply skipping a stitch, working the next stitch, leaving it on the left needle, then working the skipped stitch and slipping both stitches from the needle at the same time. There are many variations of the mock cable. The illustrations here show you step-by-step how to work the mock cable in the Cashmere Deluxe Cardigan and Hat on pages 122 and 128. Once you understand the mock cable concept, you can apply your knowledge to other variations.

To make the mock cable shown in the Mini Cable Rib chart, do the following when you get to the mock cable symbol:

1) Skip first stitch: Do not work the first stitch on your left needle. Instead, leaving the first stitch in place, knit the second stitch but do not remove it from the right needle.

2) Knit the first stitch, then remove the first and second stitches from the left needle.

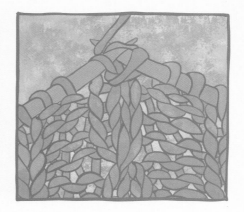

WORKING REAL CABLES

True, or real, cables (as opposed to mock cables; see left) are generally worked with a cable needle. Work across the row up to the cable crossing, then transfer the specified number of stitches to a cable needle, hold the cable needle at either the front or back of the work, work another specified group of stitches, then work the stitches from the cable needle. The two groups of stitches have exchanged places, and the result is a cable that twists to the right or the left (depending on whether the cable stitches were held in front of or behind the work) and takes on a ropelike or braided appearance. There are myriad cable variations. The illustrations here walk you step-by-step through the cable in the Cashmere Deluxe Blanket on page 118. Once you understand the cable concept, you can apply your knowledge to other variations.

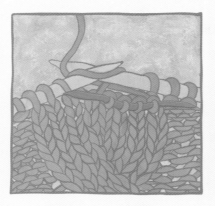 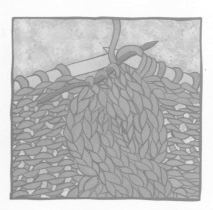

To make the first cable for the Cashmere Deluxe Blanket, work to row 3 of the body of the blanket, then to the point where the instructions tell you to slip 4 stitches to the cable needle. If you are working from the chart, do the following when you reach the cable symbol:

1) Slip 4 stitches to the cable needle and hold in front: Insert the cable needle into the next stitch on the left needle as if you were going to purl it, but instead of purling it simply transfer it to the cable needle. One at a time, repeat with the next 3 stitches on the left knitting needle. When you have transferred all 4 stitches, drop the cable needle in the front of the knitted fabric.

Knit 4: Knit the next 4 stitches on the left needle, ignoring the stitches on the cable needle.

2) Knit 4 from cable needle: Knit the stitches off the cable needle, starting with the first one you slipped and working in order.

CASHMERE DELUXE BLANKET, CARDIGAN, AND HAT

Wrapping or dressing a baby in fine-quality cashmere is, indeed, extravagant, but it also seems entirely appropriate. Whose baby doesn't deserve to be caressed in one of the softest, lightest, warmest, and most luxurious fibers available? And what better way to knit a message of I Love You and You are Special than to make this deluxe trio, or one of its pieces.

CASHMERE DELUXE BLANKET

This incredibly soft blanket features an easy eight-stitch cable. To keep the sides of the blanket straight, the cable section, which contracts from side-to-side, is worked over more stitches than the top and bottom garter-stitch borders.

SIZE

30-inch square

MATERIALS

6 skeins Joseph Galler Pashmina (50 grams/170 yards; 100% cashmere) in blush #2002

24-inch circular needle in size 4, or size needed to obtain gauge

Stitch markers

Cable needle

GAUGE

30 sts and 46 rows = 4 inches on size 4 needles in overall blanket cable pattern

MAKE A GAUGE SWATCH

In order to be sure that the blanket will turn out the size you intend, take time to make a gauge swatch. Cast on 42 stitches and work chart on page 121 as shown, including garter-stitch borders and one repeat of cable from written instructions. When the swatch measures 5 inches, BO (bind off) all stitches. Block the swatch the way you intend to block the finished blanket (see page 24). The swatch should measure 5 inches wide. Measure your row gauge over a 4-inch square section of the swatch to see if you are getting 46 rows in 4 inches. If your swatch is wider than 5 inches and you have fewer than 46 rows in 4 inches, your knitting is too loose and you should reduce the size of the needle. If your swatch is less than 5 inches wide and you have more than 46 rows in 4 inches, you are knitting too tightly and you should go up a needle size.

WORK BOTTOM BORDER

With circular needle, CO (cast on) 211 sts. Work back and forth in garter stitch (knit every row) for 15 rows. Work next row as follows: Knit 8 sts, pm (place marker), *knit

9, (knit 2 sts, inc (increase) 1 using the kf&b increase shown on page 52), repeat the instructions in the parentheses one more time, knit 4, pm; repeat the instructions beginning from the * 9 more times, and end with knit 5, pm, knit 8—you now have 231 stitches.

WORK BLANKET BODY

Begin working row 1 of the blanket cable pattern on the next row. You can work from the row-by-row instructions here, or from the chart at right, the first few rows of which are explained in the row-by-row directions.

ROWS 1, 5, AND 7 (RS, RIGHT-SIDE): K8 (knit 8; these 8 sts will be knit every row throughout to form a garter-stitch border), sl m (slip marker), k5, *sl m, p4, k8, p4, k5; repeat the instructions beginning from the * 9 more times (8 sts left on needle), sl m, k8 (these last 8 sts form the other garter-stitch border).

To work row 1 from the chart, begin at the lower right corner indicated by the "1" for the row number, knit the first 8 sts as shown for the garter-stitch border, sl m (slip m indicated by heavy dot), knit 5 sts (these are to balance the pattern and make it symmetrical), sl m, work from stitch 1 to stitch 21

(the pattern repeat as indicated by the heavy outlined box and set off by a marker at each side), then go back and repeat the sequence from stitch 1 to stitch 21 nine more times, sl m, end by knitting 8 sts for the other garter-stitch border.

ROWS 2, 4, 6, AND 8 (ALL WRONG-SIDE ROWS): K8 for garter border, *sl m, p5, k4, p8, k4; rep from * 9 more times, sl m, p5, sl m, end k8 for garter border.

To work row 2 from the chart, remember that you are working from the WS (wrong-side) of the fabric, and the symbol definitions for WS rows apply. Begin at the left side of the chart (indicated by the "2"), knit the first 8 sts as shown for the garter-stitch border (the dot symbol on the WS means knit), sl m, work from stitch 21 to stitch 1 (the pattern repeat according to the WS symbol definitions is p5, k4, p8, k4), then go back and repeat the sequence from stitch 21 to stitch 1 nine more times, sl m, p5 (the sts to balance the pattern), sl m, end k8 (for other garter-stitch border).

ROW 3 (CABLE CROSSING ROW): K8 for border, sl m, k5, *sl m, p4, sl 4 sts to cable needle (cn) and hold in front of work, knit the next 4 sts on the left needle, knit the 4 sts from cn, p4, k5; repeat the instructions beginning from the * 9 more times (8 sts left on needle), sl m, k8

BLANKET CABLE

MULTIPLE OF 21 STITCHES OVER 8 ROWS

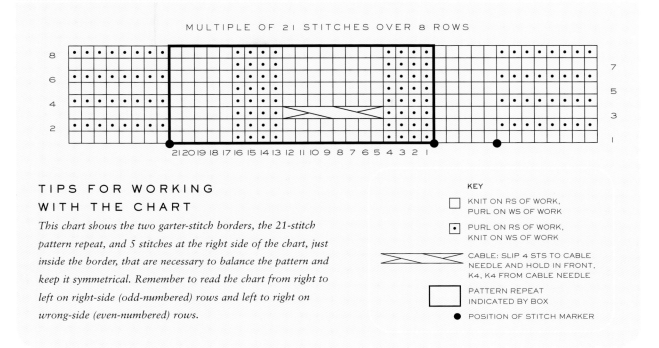

TIPS FOR WORKING
WITH THE CHART

This chart shows the two garter-stitch borders, the 21-stitch pattern repeat, and 5 stitches at the right side of the chart, just inside the border, that are necessary to balance the pattern and keep it symmetrical. Remember to read the chart from right to left on right-side (odd-numbered) rows and left to right on wrong-side (even-numbered) rows.

KEY

☐ KNIT ON RS OF WORK,
PURL ON WS OF WORK

⊡ PURL ON RS OF WORK,
KNIT ON WS OF WORK

✕ CABLE: SLIP 4 STS TO CABLE
NEEDLE AND HOLD IN FRONT,
K4, K4 FROM CABLE NEEDLE

☐ PATTERN REPEAT
INDICATED BY BOX

● POSITION OF STITCH MARKER

(these last 8 sts form the other garter-stitch border.

To work row 3 from the chart, begin at the row marked "3", k8 for border, sl m, knit 5, sl m, work from stitch 1 to stitch 21, making a cable crossing over stitches 5 to 12 as defined in the symbol key, then go back and repeat the sequence from stitch 1 to stitch 21 nine more times, sl m, end with k8 for border.

Keeping the 8 stitches at each side in garter stitch (knit every row), work in pattern until row 8 has been completed, then go back to row 1 and start the pattern over again. You will notice that all the WS rows are worked exactly the same. The RS rows are also worked alike, except for the cable crossing in row 3. (As your fabric becomes established you may find that you have memorized the pattern and do not need to keep looking at the directions or chart. Just don't forget to count your rows so you remember to cross the cables in row 3!)

Repeat the 8 rows for pattern until the piece measures about 28½" from the cast-on edge, ending with row 6 of the pattern (so that the first and last cable crossings are the same distance from the bottom and top borders). Don't worry if the measurement is not exact; you can block the blanket to the correct dimensions.

WORK TOP BORDER

To decrease back to the original number of sts, knit across the next row as follows, discarding the markers as you come to them: k8, remove m (remove marker), k5, *remove m, p4, (k2, k2tog) twice, p4, k5; repeat from * 9 more times, remove m, k8. You now have 211 sts on your needles (the same number of sts with which you began). Work 15 more rows of garter stitch. BO (bind off) all sts.

Weave in all yarn ends. Block according to the instructions on page 24. Note that after blocking the cashmere will bloom and develop a subtle fluffy halo.

CASHMERE DELUXE CARDIGAN

This classic cardigan features a mock cable twist that is worked into a simple knit 2, purl 2 rib, referred to in the pattern as a Mini Cable Rib.

SIZES

3 months, 6 months, 9 months, 12 months, 18 months, 24 months

Finished circumference, buttoned: $18^1/2$ ($20^1/2$, $22^1/2$, $24^1/2$, $28^1/2$, $30^1/2$)"

Shown in size 9 months

MATERIALS

3 (3, 3, 4, 4, 5) skeins Joseph Galler Pashmina (50 grams/ 170 yards; 100% cashmere) in blush #2002

1 pair size 2 needles, or size needed to obtain gauge

1 pair size 4 needles, or size needed to obtain gauge

Stitch markers

T-pins

Yarn needle

Five $^1/2$-inch buttons

GAUGE

32 sts and 42 rows = 4 inches in Mini Cable Rib pattern using larger needles

CHOOSE SIZE

Select a size as instructed on page 71.

MAKE GAUGE SWATCH

In order to be sure that the cardigan will turn out the size you intend, take time to make a gauge swatch. Cast on approximately 42 stitches using the larger size needles and work in Mini Cable Rib pattern from written instructions or chart for 5 inches. Bind off (BO) in pattern. (In other words, work each st in BO row as you would if you were continuing the established pattern). Block the swatch the way you intend to block the finished cardigan (see page 24). Measure your gauge over a 4-inch square section of the swatch.

MAKE BACK

CO (cast on) 74 (82, 90, 98, 114, 122) sts (stitches) with larger needles. You can work from the row-by-row instructions for the Mini Rib Cable at right, or from the chart on page 125, the first few rows of which are explained in the row-by-row directions.

ROW 1 (RS; RIGHT-SIDE): *K2, p2; repeat the instructions beginning from the * until there are only 2 sts rem (remaining) on the left needle, end k2.

To work row 1 from the chart, begin at the lower right corner indicated by the "1" for row number, work from stitch 1 to stitch 8 (the pattern repeat as indicated by the heavy outlined box), then go back and repeat the sequence from stitch 1 to stitch 8 until there are only 2 sts remaining on the left needle, end k2 (the last 2 sts balance the pattern and keep it symmetrical).

ROWS 2 AND 4 (WS; WRONG-SIDE): P2, *k2, p2; repeat the instructions beginning from the * to the end of the row.

To work rows 2 and 4 from the chart, remember that you are working from the WS of the fabric, and the symbol definitions for WS rows apply. Begin at the left side of chart (indicated by the "2"), p2, work from stitch 8 to stitch 1 (the pattern repeat according to the wrong-side symbol definitions is k2, p2, k2, p2), then go back and repeat the sequence from stitch 8 to stitch 1 to the end of the row.

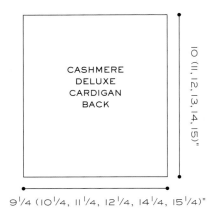

CASHMERE DELUXE CARDIGAN BACK

10 (11, 12, 13, 14, 15)"

9¼ (10¼, 11¼, 12¼, 14¼, 15¼)"

2½ (2¾, 3, 3½, 4½, 4¾)"

1½"

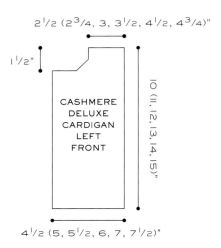

CASHMERE DELUXE CARDIGAN LEFT FRONT

10 (11, 12, 13, 14, 15)"

4½ (5, 5½, 6, 7, 7½)"

8 (9, 10, 11, 12, 13)"

6 (6½, 7, 7½, 8½, 10)"

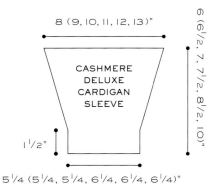

CASHMERE DELUXE CARDIGAN SLEEVE

1½"

5¼ (5¼, 5¼, 6¼, 6¼, 6¼)"

ROW 3 (MOCK CABLE ROW): *K2, p2, twist the mock cable over the next 2 sts (see illustration on page 116), p2; repeat the instructions beginning from the * until there are only 2 sts rem on the left needle, end k2.

To work row 3 from the chart, begin at the row marked "3", work from stitch 1 to stitch 8, making a mock cable twist as defined in the symbol key over stitches 5 and 6, then go back and repeat the sequence from stitch 1 to stitch 8 until there are 2 sts rem on the left needle, end k2.

Work in pattern until row 4 has been completed, then go back to row 1 and start the pattern over again. You will notice that all the WS rows are worked exactly the same.

Work in pattern until piece meas (measures) about 10 (11, 12, 13, 14, 15)" from the cast-on, ending with row 4 of pattern. BO (bind off) all sts in pattern.

MAKE LEFT FRONT

Because the 8-stitch pattern repeat represents 1 inch of knitted width, it is not possible to get the size increments necessary for the fronts by adding or removing entire repeats. Here we introduce instructions and a chart that have different starting points for different sizes.

CO 36 (40, 44, 48, 56, 60) sts with larger needles, and work in Mini Cable Rib from written instructions or from left front chart, as you prefer, paying attention to the instruction variations for different sizes.

ROW 1 (RS): *K2, p2; repeat the instructions beginning from the * until the end of row.

To work row 1 from the left front chart, begin at the lower right corner indicated by the "1" for row number; for sizes 3, 9, and 24 months, work the first 4 sts of the chart as k2, p2, then for all sizes work from stitch 1 to stitch 8 (the pattern repeat as indicated by the heavy outlined box), then go back and repeat the sequence from stitch 1 to stitch 8 to the end of the row.

ROWS 2 AND 4 (WS): *K2, p2; repeat the instructions beginning from the * to end of row.

To work rows 2 and 4 from the chart, remember that you are working from the WS of the fabric, and the symbol definitions for WS rows apply. Begin at the left side of chart (indicated by the "2") and for all sizes work from stitch 8 to stitch 1 (the pattern repeat according to the WS symbol definitions is k2, p2, k2, p2), then go back and repeat the sequence from stitch 8 to stitch 1 until there are 4 (0, 4, 0, 0, 4) sts rem; then for sizes 3, 9, and 24 months, work the 4 sts outside the repeat box as k2, p2.

CARDIGAN MINI CABLE RIB

LEFT FRONT
MULTIPLE OF 8 STS, PLUS 4
OVER 4 ROWS

RIGHT FRONT
MULTIPLE OF 8 STS, PLUS 4
OVER 4 ROWS

BACK & SLEEVES
MULTIPLE OF 8 STS, PLUS 2
OVER 4 ROWS

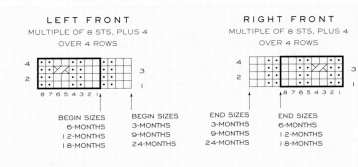

BEGIN SIZES
6-MONTHS
12-MONTHS
18-MONTHS

BEGIN SIZES
3-MONTHS
9-MONTHS
24-MONTHS

END SIZES
3-MONTHS
9-MONTHS
24-MONTHS

END SIZES
6-MONTHS
12-MONTHS
18-MONTHS

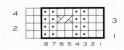

KEY

☐ KNIT ON RS OF WORK, PURL ON WS OF WORK

▪ PURL ON RS OF WORK, KNIT ON WS OF WORK

⧖ MOCK CABLE: SKIP FIRST ST, KNIT THE SECOND ST ON THE LEFT NEEDLE, THEN KNIT THE FIRST STITCH, THEN SLIP BOTH STS OFF THE NEEDLE TOGETHER

☐ PATTERN REPEAT INDICATED BY BOX

TIPS FOR WORKING WITH THE CHART

These three charts show the 8-stitch pattern repeat and any stitches required in addition to the pattern to make the design symmetrical or to create a mirror-image on two opposing garment pieces. Remember to read the charts from right to left on right-side (odd-numbered) rows and left to right on wrong-side (even-numbered) rows.

ROW 3 (MOCK CABLE ROW): For sizes 3, 9, and 24 months, work the first 4 sts of row 3 as k2, p2, then for all sizes work *k2, p2, twist the mock cable over the next 2 sts, p2; repeat the instructions beginning from the * to the end of the row.

To work row 3 from the chart, begin at the row marked "3"; for sizes 3, 9, and 24 months, work the first 4 sts of the chart as k2, p2, then for all sizes work from stitch 1 to stitch 8, making a mock cable twist as defined in the symbol key over stitches 5 and 6, then go back and repeat the sequence from stitch 1 to stitch 8 to the end of the row.

Work in pattern until piece meas about 8 1/2 (9 1/2, 10 1/2, 11 1/2, 12 1/2, 13 1/2)" from cast-on row, ending with

row 3 of pattern (you have just finished a RS row and are ready to start a WS row). Shape the neck as follows: At beg of next row (neck edge) BO 11 (11, 12, 12, 13, 14) sts, work in pattern to end—25 (29, 32, 36, 43, 46) sts rem. Work one RS row even (work across all stitches in pattern with no shaping). At beg of next WS row, BO 1 st, work in pattern to end—24 (28, 31, 35, 42, 45) sts. Work one RS row even. Repeat these last 2 rows, binding off 1 st at neck edge (at beg of the WS rows) as before, 5 (5, 7, 7, 7, 7) more times—19 (23, 24, 28, 35, 38) sts. Work even with no further shaping until piece measures 10 (11, 12, 13, 14, 15)" from beginning, ending with row 4 of pattern. BO all sts in pattern.

MAKE RIGHT FRONT

The arrangement of the stitch pattern for the right front is slightly different from that of the left front so that the pattern will form a mirror-image along the center-front cardigan opening.

CO 36 (40, 44, 48, 56, 60) sts with larger needles, and work in Mini Cable Rib from written instructions or from right front chart, as you prefer.

ROW I (RS): *P2, k2; repeat the instructions beginning from the * until the end of row.

To work row 1 from the right front chart, begin at the lower right corner indicated by the "1" for row number, work from stitch 1 to stitch

8 (the pattern repeat as indicated by the heavy outlined box), then go back and repeat the sequence from stitch 1 to stitch 8 until there are 4 (0, 4, 0, 0, 4) sts rem on the left needle, then for sizes 3, 9, and 24 months, work the last 4 sts as p2, k2

ROWS 2 AND 4 (WS): *P2, k2; repeat the instructions beginning from the * to end of row.

To work rows 2 and 4 from the chart, remember that you are working from the WS of the fabric, and the symbol definitions for WS rows apply. Begin at the left side of chart (indicated by the "2"), for sizes 3, 9, and 24 months, work the 4 sts outside the repeat box as p2, k2, then for all sizes work from stitch 8 to stitch 1 (the pattern repeat according to the WS symbol definitions is p2, k2, p2, k2), then go back and repeat the sequence from stitch 8 to stitch 1 to the end of the row.

ROW 3 (MOCK CABLE ROW): *P2, twist the mock cable over the next 2 sts, p2, k2; repeat the instructions beginning from the * until there are 4 (0, 4, 0, 0, 4) sts rem on the needle, then for sizes 3, 9, and 24 months, work the last 4 sts as p2, k2.

To work row 3 from the chart, begin at the row marked "3", work from stitch 1 to stitch 8, making a mock cable twist as defined in the symbol key over stitches 3 and 4,

then go back and repeat the sequence from stitch 1 to stitch 8 until there are 4 (0, 4, 0, 0, 4) sts rem on the needle, then for sizes 3, 9, and 24 months, work the last 4 sts as p2, k2.

Work in pattern until piece meas about 8 1/2 (9 1/2, 10 1/2, 11 1/2, 12 1/2, 13 1/2)" from cast-on row, ending with row 4 of pattern (you have just finished a WS row and are ready to start a RS row). Shape the neck as follows: At beg of next row (neck edge) BO 11 (11, 12, 12, 13, 14) sts, work in pattern to end—25 (29, 32, 36, 43, 46) sts rem. Work 1 WS row even. At beg of next RS row, BO 1 st, work in pattern to end—24 (28, 31, 35, 42, 45) sts. Work 1 WS row even. Repeat these last 2 rows, binding off 1 st at neck edge (at beg of RS rows) 5 (5, 7, 7, 7, 7) more times—19 (23, 24, 28, 35, 38) sts. Work even until piece meas 10 (11, 12, 13, 14, 15)" from beginning, ending with row 4 of pattern. BO all sts in pattern.

MAKE SLEEVES

With smaller needles, CO 42 (42, 42, 50, 50, 50) sts. Work in Mini Cable Rib according to instructions or chart for Back and Sleeves as follows:

ROWS 1-4: Work these 4 rows as for Back (instructions begin on page 123).

Work in pattern until piece meas 1 1/2" from the beginning, ending with a WS row. Change to larger needles and begin increasing

to shape sleeve. (If you make your increases inside the selvedge (edge) sts at each side, your work will have neater selvedges, and it will be easier to sew the seams together).

On the next RS row, knit 1, increase 1 by kf&b (knitting into the front and back of the same st; see page 52), work in pattern to last 2 sts, kf&b, end knit 1—44 (44, 44, 52, 52, 52) sts. (As you continue to shape the sleeve, you will work the increased stitches into the Mini Cable Rib pattern as they become established.) Work 1 WS row even. Beginning with the next RS row, increase 1 stitch at each side every other row (RS rows) 4 (7, 12, 10, 13, 13) times; then increase 1 stitch at each side every 4 rows (work 1 RS increase row followed by 3 rows without shaping) 6 (7, 6, 8, 9, 13) times—64 (72, 80, 88, 96, 104) sts. Work even in pattern until piece meas 6 (6 1/2, 7, 7 1/2, 8 1/2, 10)" from beginning. BO all sts in pattern. Make a second sleeve the same as the first.

SEW SEAMS

Using the mattress stitch and following the illustration labeled Bind Off to Bind Off on page 23, sew the fronts and back together at the shoulder seams. Lay the sweater out flat, right side up, with the shoulder seams in the center, and the fronts and back extending above and below them. Place pins or removable markers 4 (4 1/2, 5, 5 1/2, 6, 6 1/2)" from the shoulder seams along each side of the fronts and back. Fold each sleeve in half the long way and mark the midpoint of the top edge of the sleeve. Pin the sleeve to the body between the markers at front and back, matching the midpoint sleeve marker to the shoulder seam. Sew the top of the sleeve to the body using the mattress stitch labeled Rows to Bind Off. As you work, tug along the length of the seam to stretch out the sewn stitches so that the seam will lie flat and not pucker. Attach the second sleeve in the same way. Sew sleeve and side seams using the mattress stitch labeled Rows to Rows.

MAKE BUTTONHOLE BAND

Traditionally, girls' cardigans have buttonholes on the right front and boys' cardigans have buttonholes on the left front. To make this sweater unisex, buttonholes can be worked on both front bands. The buttons, sewn on top of the unused button-holes, can be moved from one side to the other as necessary.

Using removable markers or scraps of waste yarn, mark the posi-tion of 5 buttonholes on the right front for a girl, or left front for a boy (or both sides for a unisex version), the lowest buttonhole 1/2" up from the bottom edge, and the highest 1/2" below the beginning of the

neck shaping, with the others evenly spaced in between.

Make a buttonhole band on the side that you have marked as follows: With RS facing, beginning at the lower edge of the right front or neck edge of the left front, using smaller needles, pick up and knit 52 (56, 60, 64, 68, 72) sts from the bottom edge to the beginning of the neck shaping (see page 81). On the next row, establish k2, p2 rib as follows: *K2, p2; repeat from * to end of row. All rows of the bands will be worked in this same pattern. On the next row (RS), maintaining the k2, p2 rib as established, make a buttonhole at each marked position as follows: *Work in pattern to marker, yo (yarnover; see page 53), k2tog (knit 2 together; see page 53); repeat from * until 5 buttonholes have been com-pleted, work in pattern to end of row. (On the following row, knit or purl the yo's as dictated by the pat-tern.) Work in k2, p2 rib pattern for 3 more rows. BO all sts in pattern.

MAKE BUTTON BAND

Work a button band on the other side of the front opening the same as the buttonhole band, but without the buttonholes: 5 rows of k2, p2 rib before binding off.

MAKE NECKBAND

With RS facing and smaller needles, beginning at the join between the right front and its front band, pick

up and knit 62 (70, 78, 78, 78, 86) stitches evenly spaced around neck opening, ending where the left front joins the left front band. Work the next row (WS of garment) as follows to establish the k2, p2 rib pattern: *P2, k2; repeat from * to last 2 sts, end p2. Work the next 4 rows as follows:

ROWS 1 AND 3 (RS): *K2, p2; repeat from * to last 2 sts, end k2.

ROWS 2 AND 4 (WS): *P2, k2; repeat from * to last 2 sts, end p2.

When these 4 rows have been completed, BO all sts in pattern.

FINISHING

Weave in ends. Block according to the instructions on page 24. Note that after blocking the cashmere will bloom; it will develop a subtle fluffy halo. Sew on buttons.

CASHMERE DELUXE HAT

SIZES

12½ (14, 16)" circumference
when hat is slightly stretched,
to fit newborn to 6 months
(6 to 12 months, 12 to 24 months)

Shown in size 6 to 12 months

MATERIALS

2 (2, 2) skeins Joseph Galler
Pashmina (50 grams/170 yards;
100% cashmere) in blush #2002

12-inch circular needle or set of
4 double-pointed needles in size 4,
or size needed to obtain gauge

Yarn needle

GAUGE

32 sts and 42 rows = 4 inches
on size 4 needles in Mini Cable Rib
pattern worked in the round

This hat is knit in the round and features the same mock cable as the *Cashmere Deluxe Cardigan*.

The shaping at the top of the hat is achieved using a p2tog (purl 2 together) decrease. This is worked by inserting the right needle into the first 2 stitches on the left needle and purling them together as if they were one stitch, just as the k2tog (knit 2 together) decrease introduced on page 53 is worked by knitting two stitches as if they were one.

Because the hat is such a small project, it doesn't make sense to do a true gauge swatch. Instead, simply start knitting the hat. After you have finished a few inches, measure your gauge. If it is correct, continue knitting. If it isn't, determine whether you want to start over with a different size needle. The pattern will work even if you're not knitting exactly to the recommended gauge, although you should try to be fairly close.

This pattern includes three sizes. The first number given refers to size newborn to 6 months, and the numbers in parentheses refer to sizes 6 to 12 months and 12 to 24 months, in that order. To make it easier to follow the instructions, choose the size you want to make and go through the pattern and highlight all of the numbers that apply to that size. If you do not want to write directly in the book, photocopy the instructions and highlight the copy.

MAKE BRIM

Cast on 88 (96, 112) sts (stitches). Join for working in the round, taking care not to twist sts. Place a marker at the beginning of the round (see page 100 for preparing to work in the round). Work Mini Cable Rib in the Round as explained below. Because you are working in the round, you will always be working from the RS (right-side) of the fabric.

ROUNDS 1, 2, AND 4 (ALL THE SAME): *K2, p2; repeat from * to end of round.

ROUND 3 (MOCK CABLE ROUND): *K2, p2, twist the mock cable over the next 2 sts (see instructions on page 116), p2; repeat from * to end of round.

Repeat these 4 rounds for pattern, and work in pattern for 2 inches, ending with round 4. These first 2 inches will form the brim of the hat.

MAKE BODY OF HAT

In order for the RS of the brim to show when it is folded back, you need to reverse the RS and WS (wrong-side) of your work. Turn the piece inside out so that the RS of the mock cables you have worked so far are on the inside of the cylinder you have made. Beg the Mini Cable Rib in the Round pattern, working k2 over the p2 sections, and p2 over the k2 sections as they face you. Be sure to place the mock cable twist over the ones on the brim (this will be on p2 section as the brim faces you) so that the pattern will match up when the brim is turned up. Work until piece meas (measures) 8 (9, 10)" from the beginning.

SHAPE AND FINISH

Work a decrease round every 4th round (1 decrease round followed by 3 rounds with no decreasing) as follows:

ROUND 1: *K2, p2tog, k2, p2; repeat from * to end of round—77 (84, 98) sts rem (remain).

ROUNDS 2, 3, AND 4: *K2, p1, k2, p2; repeat from * to end of round

ROUND 5: *K2, p1, k2, p2tog; repeat from * to end of round—66 (72, 84) sts rem.

ROUNDS 6, 7, AND 8: *K2, p1, k2, p1; repeat from * to end of round.

ROUND 9: *K2, p1, k2tog, p1; repeat from * to end of round—55 (60, 70) sts rem.

ROUNDS 10, 11, AND 12: *K2, p1, k1, p1; repeat from * to end of round.

ROUND 13: *K2tog, p1, k1, p1; repeat from * to end of round—44 (48, 56) sts rem.

ROUND 14: *K1, p1; repeat from * to end of round.

ROUND 15: K2tog around—22 (24, 28) sts rem.

ROUND 16: Knit all stitches.

ROUND 17: K2tog around—11 (12, 14) sts.

Cut the working yarn, leaving a 10-inch tail. Thread the tail onto a yarn needle, then through rem sts and pull tightly like a drawstring to close top of hat. Weave in all yarn tails. Block as instructed on page 24. Note that after blocking the cashmere will bloom and develop a subtle fluffy halo.

Make a pom-pom according to the instructions on page 37. Fold up brim.

ARAN PULLOVER

SIZES

3 months, 6 months,
9 months, 12 months,
18 months, 24 months

Finished chest circumference:
19 (21, 22¹/2, 24¹/2, 26, 28)"

Shown in size 12 months

MATERIALS

4 (5, 5, 6, 7, 8) skeins Russi Sales
Heirloom Easy Care 8 Ply (50
grams/107 yards; 100% machine-
washable wool) in light blue #780
or olive green #799

1 pair size 6 needles, or size
needed to obtain gauge

1 pair size 8 needles, or size
needed to obtain gauge

Cable needle

2 stitch holders

T-pins

Yarn needle

Four ¹/2-inch buttons

GAUGE

17 stitches and 28 rows = 4"
in seed stitch on larger needles

The exact origin of the Aran pullover is not known. There is convincing evidence that this heavily textured sweater, always a cable showcase, was born in the early- to mid-20th century in Ireland as an outgrowth of traditional fisherman's gansey knitting and as a means of generating export income for knitters living on the Aran Islands. Today, the term Aran is used loosely to describe nearly any cabled sweater. Our adaptation of the Aran tradition combines real and mock cables with seed stitch and buttons at the shoulder to make dressing and undressing easy. Note that in this pattern instructions for seed stitch are provided in a Stitch Guide (see page 132). It is very common to include this kind of stitch information at the beginning of a pattern so that the knitter can refer back to it easily.

CHOOSE SIZE

This pattern includes six sizes. The first number given refers to size 3 months, and the numbers in paren- theses refer to sizes 6 months, 9 months, 12 months, 18 months, and 24 months, in that order. To make it easier to follow the instructions, choose the size you want to make and go through the pattern and highlight all of the numbers that apply to that size. If you do not want to write directly in the book, photocopy the instructions and highlight the copy.

MAKE A GAUGE SWATCH

Cast on 22 stitches and work seed stitch over an even number of stitches for 5 inches. Block the swatch the way you intend to block the finished garment (see page 24). Measure your gauge over a 4-inch square section of the swatch. If your swatch has fewer stitches and rows per inch than the project gauge, your knitting is too loose and you should reduce the size of the needle. If your swatch has more stitches and rows than the project gauge, your knitting is too tight and you should go up a needle size.

START BACK

With smaller needles, CO (cast on) 39 (43, 47, 51, 55, 59) sts. Work in St st for 2 rows. Then work seed stitch over an odd number of sts for 5 rows. In next row (WS; wrong side) increase 17 sts evenly across as follows: Work seed stitch as est (established) over 3 (5, 7, 9, 11, 13) sts, *kf&b (knit into front and back of next st to increase 1; see page 52), p1; repeat from * 15 more times, kf&b, work seed st as est over 3 (5, 7, 9, 11, 13) sts—56 (60, 64, 68, 72, 76) sts.

ESTABLISH CABLES AND SEED STITCH

Change to larger needles, and set up pattern as follows: Work 3 (5, 7, 9, 11, 13) sts in seed stitch as est, pm (place marker), work row 1 of Aran Cables chart over center 50 sts, pm, work 3 (5, 7, 9, 11, 13) sts in seed st as est. When you have completed row 8 of the chart, go back to the beginning and repeat the pattern from row 1. Work in pattern as est until piece meas (measures) 10 (11, 12, 13, 14, 15)" from the beginning with the St st edge rolled up, ending with a WS row.

On the next RS (right-side) row, change to smaller needles and work across all sts in seed stitch, dec (decreasing) 17 sts as follows: Work seed stitch as est over 3 (5, 7, 9, 11, 13) sts, *work 2 sts together in pattern (either k2tog or p2tog, depending on what the next st needs to be in seed stitch), work 1 st in seed stitch; repeat from * 15 more times, work 2 sts together in pattern, work seed stitch as est over 3

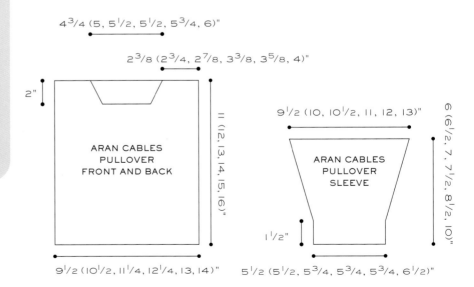

ARAN CABLES

WORKED OVER CENTER 50 STITCHES

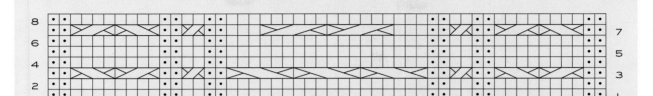

TIPS FOR WORKING WITH THE CHART

For this pattern, refer to the symbol key for directions on how to work the cables. All the cable crossings occur on rows 3 and 7, and all the WS rows are worked exactly the same. For general instructions on how to work cables, see page 117. Remember to read the charts from right to left on right-side (odd-numbered) rows and left to right on wrong-side (even-numbered) rows.

Our chart shows a stitch marker at each end of the 50-stitch cable section to separate it from the seed stitch sections at each side. You may find it helpful to use additional markers within the cable section to indicate the individual cables and the purl stitch columns. Once the pattern becomes established, you may remove the extra markers if you no longer need them.

KEY

☐ KNIT ON RS OF WORK, PURL ON WS OF WORK

⊡ PURL ON RS OF WORK, KNIT ON WS OF WORK

SLIP 1 ST TO CABLE NEEDLE (CN) AND HOLD IN BACK, K1, K1 FROM CN

SLIP 2 STS TO CN AND HOLD IN BACK, K2, K2 FROM CN

SLIP 2 STS TO CN AND HOLD IN FRONT, K2, K2 FROM CN

SLIP 3 STS TO CN AND HOLD IN BACK, K3, K3 FROM CN

SLIP 3 STS TO CN AND HOLD IN FRONT, K3, K3 FROM CN

(5, 7, 9, 11, 13) sts—39 (43, 47, 51, 55, 59) sts. Work in seed stitch for 6 more rows, ending with a RS row. Work 2 rows in St st beginning with a WS row (purl 1 row, knit 1 row). BO (bind off) all sts.

FRONT

Work same as back until piece meas 9 (10, 11, 12, 13, 14)" with the St st bottom edge rolled up, and end having just completed a WS row. Beginning with the next RS row, shape neck as follows: Work 19 (20, 21, 23, 24, 25) sts (these will be the left shoulder stitches as the sweater is worn), join a second ball of yarn and BO the center 18 (20, 22, 22, 24, 26) sts (these are the center front neck stitches), and work the rem (remaining) 19 (20, 21, 23, 24, 25) sts to end (these are the right shoul-der stitches when worn). Now you will work only on the sts for the right shoulder. The sts for the left shoulder will stay on the needle, but you will ignore them for now. BO stitches in the center will provide enough separation between the 2 sides so you can work each inde-pendently. Working only on the sts for the right shoulder, where your second ball of yarn is connected,

turn the work around and work 19 (20, 21, 23, 24, 25) sts in pattern. Turn again, BO 2 sts at the beginning of the next RS row, and work in pattern to end—17 (18, 19, 21, 22, 23) sts rem. Continue in this manner, working a WS row, then a RS row with 2 sts BO at the beginning of the row, until there are 13 (14, 15, 17, 18, 19) sts rem for this shoulder. Work even (without any further shaping), until piece meas 10 (11, 12, 13, 14, 15)" from the beginning with the bottom edge rolled, ending with a WS row. Place sts on a holder.

Now you will work on the sts for the other side, using the first ball of yarn, which is still connected to the left shoulder sts. Turn the work, BO 2 sts at the beginning of the next WS row, work in pattern to end—17 (18, 19, 21, 22, 23) sts. Turn again and work across all sts

in pattern. Continue to BO 2 sts at the beginning of each WS row, work to end, then work a RS row without shaping, until there are 13 (14, 15, 17, 18, 19) sts rem. Work even until this shoulder meas 10 (11, 12, 13, 14, 15)" from the beginning with the bottom edge rolled, ending with a WS row. Place sts on holder. (As you have seen, because you can only BO sts at the beginning of a row, neck shaping is worked by BO sts at the beginning of RS rows for one side of the neck, and at the beginning of WS rows for the other side.)

MAKE SLEEVES

With smaller needles, CO 23 (23, 25, 25, 25, 27) sts. Work in St st for 2 rows. Work in seed stitch over an odd number of sts for 9 rows. Change to larger needles and begin increasing to shape sleeve. (If you make your increases inside the selvedge (edge) sts at each side, your work will have neater selvedges, and it will be easier to sew the seams together.)

On the next RS row, work 1 st in pattern, increase 1 by kf&b, work in pattern to last 2 sts, kf&b,

work last st—25 (25, 27, 27, 27, 29) sts. As you continue to shape the sleeve, you will work the increased stitches into the seed st pattern as they become established. Work one WS row even. Beginning with the next RS row, increase 1 st at each side every other row (RS rows) 2 (1, 0, 0, 0, 0) times; then increase 1 st at each side every 4 rows (work 1 RS increase row followed by three rows without shaping) 6 (8, 9, 10, 12, 13) times—41 (43, 45, 47, 51, 55) sts. Work even in seed stitch until piece meas 6 (6½, 7, 7½, 8½, 10)" with St st section rolled up. BO all sts. Make a second sleeve the same as the first.

FINISH FRONT NECK

With smaller needles and RS facing, join yarn at the beginning of the front neck curve, starting at the base of the endmost shoulder stitch on the holder, and pick up 22 (24, 26, 26, 28, 30) sts evenly around front of neck to the base of the other shoulder stitch holder (see illustration on page 81). Work in seed stitch over an even number of sts for 7 rows. Work in St st for 2 rows, beginning with a purl row. BO all sts.

WORK BUTTON BANDS AT SHOULDERS

Slip 13 (14, 15, 17, 18, 19) sts from holder for left shoulder to smaller needle and join yarn at armhole edge, ready to work a RS row. With smaller needles, work across 13 (14, 15, 17, 18, 19) sts in seed stitch, then pick up and knit 5 sts along side of seed stitch section of front neckband (do not pick up any sts along the side of the St st section)—18 (19, 20, 22, 23, 24) sts. Work 2 rows seed stitch across all sts. On the next row (WS), make 2 buttonholes as follows: Work 3 sts in seed stitch, work 2 sts together to decrease 1 st (k2tog or p2tog, as dictated by the seed stitch pattern), yo (yarnover, see page 53), work 5 sts seed stitch, work 2 sts together to decrease 1 st, yo, work in seed stitch to end of row. Work 4 more rows seed stitch. Work 2 rows St st, beginning with a knit row. BO all sts.

Slip 13 (14, 15, 17, 18, 19) sts from holder for right shoulder to smaller needle, ready to work a RS row. With smaller needles, join yarn at edge of front neckband, pick up and knit 5 sts along side of seed stitch section of front neckband (do not pick up any sts along the side of the St st section), then work across 13 (14, 15, 17, 18, 19) sts of shoulder in seed stitch—18 (19, 20, 22, 23, 24) sts. Work 2 rows seed stitch across all sts. On the next row (WS), make 2 buttonholes as follows:

Work 6 (7, 8, 10, 11, 12) sts in seed stitch, yo, work 2 sts together, work 5 sts seed stitch, yo, work 2 sts together, work 3 sts seed stitch. Work 4 more rows seed stitch. Work 2 rows St st, beginning with a knit row. BO all sts.

FINISHING

Overlap the buttonhole seed st sections of the front over the plain seed stitch section of the back and sew the 2 layers together at the sides. Lay the sweater out flat, RS up, with the neck opening in the center, and the front and back extending above and below it. Place removable markers 4¾ (5, 5¼, 5½, 6, 6½)" down from the center of the shoulder overlap along each side of the fronts and back. Fold each sleeve in half the long way and mark the midpoint of the top edge of the sleeve. Pin the sleeves to the body between the markers at front and back, matching the midpoint sleeve marker to the center of the shoulder overlap. Sew the sleeves to the body using the mattress stitch labeled Rows to Bind Off on page 23. As you work, tug along the length of the seam to stretch out the sewn stitches so that the seam will lie flat and not pucker. Sew sleeve and side seams following the mattress stitch illustration on page 45. Block according to the instructions on page 24. Sew on 2 buttons at each shoulder underneath the buttonholes.

MOMMY SWEATER

This sweater was designed to see mom through pregnancy and to be worn after the baby's birth. It is generously oversized and stretches easily to accommodate a growing belly. It is made out of washable wool so that it can be laundered easily and, if necessary, often. Each time it is washed, it can be blocked back into its original shape. The allover rib stitch is quick and easy to knit.

SIZES

Extra-small, small, medium, large, extra-large

Finished chest circumference: $41^{1}/_{2}$ ($43^{1}/_{2}$, $48^{1}/_{2}$, 53, $55^{1}/_{2}$)"

Shown in size medium

MATERIALS

13 (14, 15, 17, 18) skeins Jaeger Matchmaker Merino Aran (50 grams/90 yards; 100% machine-washable wool) in English rose #799

1 pair size 6 needles, or size needed to obtain gauge

16-inch circular needle in size 6, or size needed to obtain gauge, for neck finishing

1 pair size 8 knitting needles, or size needed to obtain gauge

Stitch marker

T-pins

Yarn needle

GAUGE

17 stitches and 24 rows = 4" on larger needles in Garter Rib

STITCH GUIDE

GARTER RIB
(worked over multiple of 5 plus 3)
ROW 1 (RS, RIGHT-SIDE):
*P3, k2; repeat from * to last 3 sts, end p3.
ROW 2: Purl all sts.
Repeat these 2 rows for pattern.

CHOOSE SIZE

This pattern includes five sizes. The first number given refers to size extra-small, and the numbers in parentheses refer to sizes small, medium, large, and extra-large, in that order. To make it easier to follow the instructions, choose the size you want to make and go through the pattern and highlight all of the numbers that apply to that size.

MAKE A GAUGE SWATCH

Cast on 23 stitches and work in Garter Rib pattern for 5 inches. Block the swatch the way you intend to block the finished pullover (see page 24). Measure your gauge over a 4-inch square section of the swatch. If your swatch has fewer stitches and rows per inch than the project gauge, your knitting is too loose and you should reduce the size of the needle. If your swatch has more stitches and rows than the project gauge, your knitting is too tight and you should go up a needle size.

MAKE BACK

With smaller needles, CO (cast on) 88 (93, 103, 113, 118) sts. Work in Garter Rib stitch for 3". Change to larger needles and continue working in pattern until piece meas (measures) 17 ($17^{1}/_{2}$, 18, $18^{1}/_{2}$, 19)" from cast-on, and end having just completed a WS (wrong-side) row. Beginning with the next RS (right-side) row, shape underarms as follows: BO (bind off) 5 sts at the beginning of the next 2 rows—78 (83, 93, 103, 108) sts rem (remain). Continue in pattern as established until piece meas $26^{1}/2$ (27, $27^{1}/2$, 28, $28^{1}/2$)" from beginning. BO all sts.

MAKE FRONT

Work same as back until piece meas $24^{1}/2$ (25, $25^{1}/2$, 26, $26^{1}/2$)" from the beginning, and end having just completed a WS row—78 (83, 93, 103, 108) sts rem. Beginning with the next RS row, shape neck as follows: Work 31 (33, 38, 42, 44) sts (these will be the left shoulder edge as the sweater is worn), join second ball of yarn, BO center 16 (17, 17, 19, 20) sts, work the rem 31 (33, 38, 42,

44) sts to end (these are the right shoulder stitches when worn). Now you will work only on the sts for the right shoulder. The sts for the left shoulder will stay on the needle, but you will ignore them for now. The BO sts in the center will provide enough separation between the two sides so you can work each independently. Working only on the sts for the right shoulder, where your second ball of yarn is connected, turn the work around and work the 31 (33, 38, 42, 44) sts in pattern. Turn again, BO 1 st at the beginning of the next RS row, and work in pattern to end—30 (32, 37, 41, 43) sts rem. Continue in this manner, working WS row, then a RS row, with 1 st BO at the beginning of the RS rows, until there are 26 (28, 33, 37, 39) sts rem for this shoulder. Work even (without any further shaping), until piece meas $26^{1}/2$ (27,

$27^{1}/2$, 28, $28^{1}/2$)" from the beginning. BO all sts.

Now you will work on the sts for the other side, using the first ball of yarn, which is still connected to the left shoulder sts. Turn the work, BO 1 st at the beginning of the next WS row, work in pattern to end—30 (32, 37, 41, 43) sts. Turn again and work across all sts in pattern. Continue to BO 1 st at the beginning of each WS row, work to end, then work a RS row without shaping, until 26 (28, 33, 37, 39) sts rem. Work even until piece meas $26^{1}/2$ (27, $27^{1}/2$, 28, $28^{1}/2$)" from the beginning. BO all sts.

(As you have seen, because you can only BO sts at the beginning of a row, neck shaping is worked by BO sts at the beginning of RS rows for one side of the neck, and at the beginning of WS rows for the other side.)

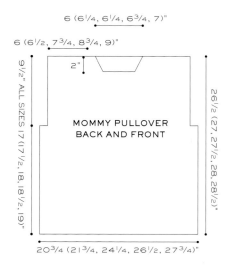

6 ($6^{1}/4$, $6^{1}/4$, $6^{3}/4$, 7)"

6 ($6^{1}/2$, $7^{3}/4$, $8^{3}/4$, 9)"

$9^{1}/2$" ALL SIZES 17 ($17^{1}/2$, 18, $18^{1}/2$, 19)"

2"

MOMMY PULLOVER
BACK AND FRONT

$26^{1}/2$ (27, $27^{1}/2$, 28, $28^{1}/2$)"

$20^{3}/4$ ($21^{3}/4$, $24^{1}/4$, $26^{1}/2$, $27^{3}/4$)"

18 ($18^{1}/2$, $19^{1}/4$, $19^{3}/4$, $20^{1}/4$)"

MOMMY
PULLOVER
SLEEVE

14 ($15^{1}/2$, 16, $16^{1}/2$, 17)"

$2^{1}/2$"

$7^{3}/4$ ($7^{3}/4$, 9, 9, 9)"

MAKE SLEEVES

With smaller needles, CO 33 (33, 38, 38, 38) sts. Work in Garter Rib pattern until piece meas 2$^{1}/_{2}$".

Change to larger needles and begin increasing to shape sleeve. (If you make your increases inside the selvedge (edge) sts at each side, your work will have neater selvedges, and it will be easier to sew the seams together.)

On the next RS row, work 1 st in pattern, increase 1 by kf&b (knit into the front and back of the same st; see page 52), work in pattern to last 2 sts, kf&b, work last st—35 (35, 40, 40, 40) sts. As you continue to shape the sleeve, you will work the increased stitches into the Garter Rib pattern as they become established. Work one WS row even. Beginning with the next RS row, increase 1 st at each side every other row (RS rows) 15 (11, 6, 3, 2) times; then every 4 rows (work 1 RS increase row followed by 3 rows without shaping) 8 (12, 15, 18, 19) times—81 (81, 82, 82, 82) sts. Work even in pattern until piece meas 14 (15$^{1}/_{2}$, 16, 16$^{1}/_{2}$, 17)" from beginning, and end having just completed a WS row. Beginning with the next RS row, shape sleeve cap as follows: BO 1 st at beg of next 10 rows—71 (71, 72, 72, 72) sts. BO all sts.

MAKE NECKBAND

Sew shoulder seams following mattress stitch illustration labeled Bind Off to Bind Off on page 23. With smaller circular needle and RS of garment facing you, beginning at the left shoulder seam, pick up and knit 68 (72, 72, 76, 80) sts evenly around neck opening as follows (see page 81): 13 (14, 14, 14, 15) sts from left shoulder seam to sts BO for front neck, 16 (17, 17, 19, 20) BO front neck sts, 13 (14, 14, 14, 15) sts from front neck to right shoulder seam, 26 (27, 27, 29, 30) BO sts across back neck. Join for working in the round and place a stitch marker to indicate the beginning of the round (see page 100). Work all rounds in k2, p2 rib as follows: *K2, p2; repeat from * to end of round. When neckband meas 3", BO all sts in rib pattern. (In other words, as you work each stitch in the BO round in preparation for binding it off, work the stitch as you would if you were continuing the k2, p2 rib pattern.)

FINISHING

Lay the sweater out flat, RS up, with the neck opening in the center, and the front and back extending above and below it. Fold each sleeve in half the long way and mark the midpoint of the top edge of the sleeve using a pin or removable stitch marker. Pin the sleeve to the body, matching the midpoint sleeve marker to shoulder seam, and matching the shaped sides of the sleeve cap to the stitches bound off on the body for armhole shaping. Sew the top of the sleeve to the body using the mattress stitch, following the Rows to Bind Off illustration on page 23. As you work, tug along the length of the seam to stretch out the sewn stitches so that the seam will lie flat and not pucker. Attach the second sleeve in the same way. Sew sleeve and side seams using the Rows to Rows mattress stitch. Block according to the instructions on page 24.

THE POSSIBILITIES OF KNITTING ARE TRULY INFINITE, AND IN
THIS CHAPTER WE INTRODUCE YOU TO A FEW NONTRADITIONAL
PROJECTS THAT MAY STRETCH YOUR IMAGINATION AND EXPAND
YOUR CONCEPT OF WHAT CAN BE ACHIEVED.

EXPLORING THE
POSSIBILITIES

chapter 8

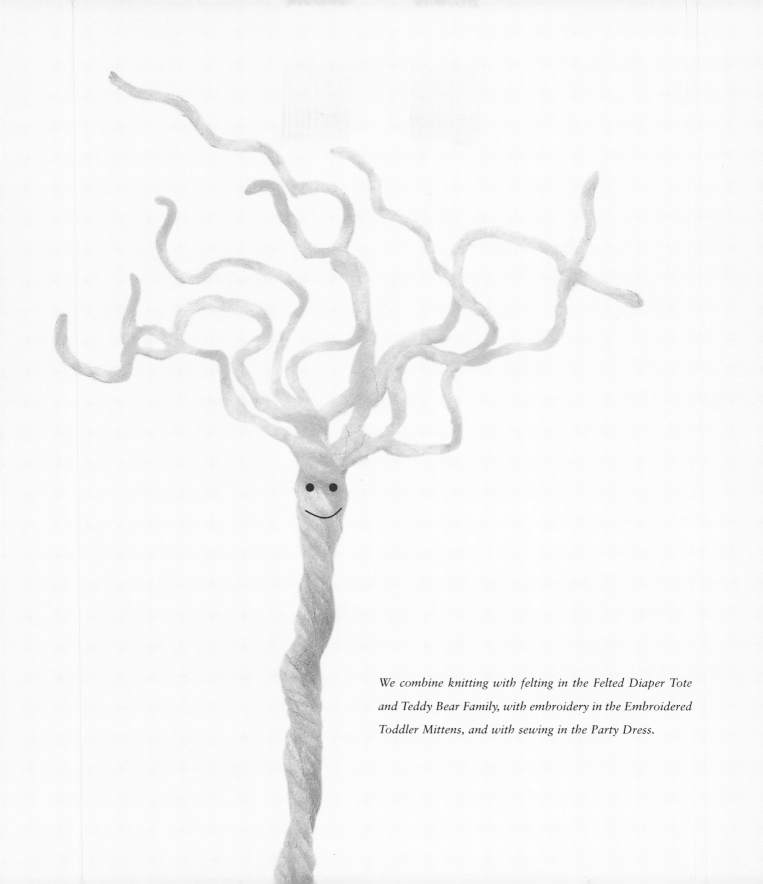

We combine knitting with felting in the *Felted Diaper Tote* and *Teddy Bear Family*, with embroidery in the *Embroidered Toddler Mittens*, and with sewing in the *Party Dress*.

17" high x 18" wide x 7" deep before felting; approximately 11" high x 15" wide x 5$^{1}/_{2}$" deep after felting

MATERIALS

Classic Elite Yarns Montera (100 grams/127 yards; 50% llama, 50% wool)

BAG #1:

Main Color (MC):
5 skeins black cherry #3853

Contrast Color (CC):
3 skeins pumpkin #3885

BAG #2:

Main Color (MC):
5 skeins morel #3811

Contrast Color (CC):
3 skeins dark charcoal #3875

1 pair size 10$^{1}/_{2}$ needles, or size needed to obtain gauge

Yarn needle

T-pins

15" x 5$^{1}/_{2}$" piece of heavy plastic, needlepoint canvas or cardboard, to keep the base of the bag rigid and flat (optional)

6$^{1}/_{2}$" x 16" piece of fabric, sewing needle, and matching thread, for lining bottom of bag (optional)

GAUGE

14 sts and 22 rows = 4" on size 10$^{1}/_{2}$ needles in seed stitch before felting

After felting, stitch gauge (width) will shrink about 17%; row gauge (length) will shrink about 35%

FELTED DIAPER TOTE

Making this bag is a simple matter of knitting eight seed-stitch rectangles (a base, a front and a back, two sides, one large pocket, and two side pockets), plus two straps, sewing them altogether into a bag shape, then felting in the washing machine. When the wool fibers in the yarn are subjected to changes in water temperature and agitation in the machine, they naturally and permanently grab onto each other, thus shrinking the bag and making it strong and impermeable. The pieces of the bag are knitted in seed stitch for thickness and durability and sewn together before felting so that they will all shrink and felt at the same rate.

STITCH GUIDE

SEED STITCH
(over odd number of sts):
ALL ROWS: *K1, p1; repeat from * to last st, end k1.

MAKE GAUGE SWATCH

Start by making one of the side pocket pieces, and check the gauge when finished. Because this project does not need to "fit," you don't have to match this gauge exactly— just try to get close.

If you knit more loosely than the specified gauge, your bag may take longer to felt down to the finished size. If you knit more tightly than the intended gauge, your bag may not turn out the correct size. If you are not knitting to gauge, it is possible that you will require more yarn than specified.

MAKE BASE

In MC (main color), CO (cast on) 63 sts (stitches). Work in Seed st for 8$^{1}/_{2}$". BO (bind off) all sts.

MAKE FRONT AND BACK

In MC, CO 63 sts. Work in Seed st for 17". BO all sts. Make a second piece the same size.

MAKE SIDES

In MC, CO 25 sts. Work in Seed st for 17". BO all sts. Make a second side piece the same size.

MAKE SIDE POCKETS

In CC (contrast color), CO 25 sts. Work in Seed st for 11$^{1}/_{2}$". BO all sts. Make a second side pocket the same size.

MAKE LARGE FRONT POCKET

In CC, CO 43 sts. Work in Seed st for 10". BO all sts.

MAKE HANDLES

In CC, CO 93 sts. Work in Seed st for 2". BO all sts. Make a second handle the same size.

SEW BAG PIECES TOGETHER

Pin the large pocket to the front, $3^1/2$" down from the top edge and about 3" in from each side. Using a yarn needle and an overcast stitch (see page 23), sew the pocket to the front piece along 3 sides, leaving the top of the pocket open. Pin the small side pockets to the side panels with the lower edges even, and attach with an overcast stitch. Sew the front, back, and side pieces together using the overcast stitch, catching the edges of the side pockets in the seams for extra durability. Sew the base of the bag to the front, back, and sides using the overcast stitch. Pin a handle to each of the top edges of front and back, with the ends of each handle about 8" apart, and overlapping the front and back by about $1^1/2$", as shown in the photograph. Attach each handle with small, firm overcast stitches.

FELT THE BAG

To felt the bag, place it in a pillow-case tied tightly closed (the pillowcase will prevent the bag from getting caught in machine parts). Place the pillowcase in your washing machine along with a few old towels (to provide extra agitation and balance the load) and about one-fourth the amount of laundry detergent you would use for a normal load. Set the machine for a 10-minute hot wash cycle and a cold rinse. When the wash and rinse cycles are complete, check the bag for felting progress. If the knitted stitches have shrunk and adhere to each other and the fabric appears dense and even, with no light shining through it, the felting is complete. If it has not sufficiently felted, return the bag to the pillow-case and washer and repeat the wash and rinse cycles, checking every 1–2 minutes, depending on how close your bag is to being com-pletely felted. Felting is not an exact science. The speed at which your bag felts will depend upon the level of agitation in your washing machine, the type of water you have, and the type of detergent you use. It is impossible to reverse the felting process so it is best to tread carefully by checking frequently until you are satisfied with your results. When ready, take the bag out of the pillowcase and stretch and pull to the finished dimensions given at the beginning of the instruc-tions. Lay the bag on its side to dry, turning it over occasionally to speed up the process. If you have a box the correct shape and size to use as a drying form (approximately 11" high x 15" wide x $5^1/2$" deep), place the bag upside-down over the box and allow to dry.

When the bag is dry, place a heavy piece of plastic, needlepoint canvas or cardboard in the bottom to form a flat base. If you are lining the bottom, trim the lining fabric to 1" longer and wider than the finished bottom, turn the raw edges under $1/2$" on all four sides, and using a sewing needle and thread, tack the fabric securely to the bottom of the bag.

1 skein Muench Esprit (50 grams/
88 yards; 100% nylon) in pink #1
and size 10 needles

1 skein Muench Cotton Velours
(50 grams/146 yards; 100% cotton)
in blue #25 and size 5 needles

1 skein Reynolds Lopi (100 grams/
110 yards; 100% Icelandic wool)
in brown tweed #167 and size 10
needles

1 skein Reynolds Lopi (100 grams/
110 yards; 100% Icelandic wool) in
tan #86 and size 10 needles (shown
felted)

1 skein Koigu Premium Merino
(50 grams/175 yards; 100% wool) in
purple #1013 and size 3 needles

1 skein Classic Elite Waterspun
(50 grams/138 yards; 100% felted
Merino wool) in celery #5036 and
size 7 needles (shown felted and
unfelted)

1 skein Reynolds Turnberry Tweed
(100 grams/220 yards; 100% wool)
in magenta #66 and size 7 needles

Yarn needle

Stitch holders

3–4 yards of embroidery yarn
or scrap yarn, per bear, for
embroidering face and paws

Handful or more (depending on
size of bear) clean, raw wool;
polyester fiberfill; or yarn scraps,
for stuffing bear

GAUGE

Use needle size and gauge recommended on the label of chosen yarn.

TEDDY BEAR FAMILY

This project demonstrates not only how adorable a knitted teddy bear can be, but also the impact of gauge on finished size and the effects of felting. The eight members of the extended bear family shown here were all made following the exact same instructions. Their different sizes are the result of differences in the yarn and needle sizes, and because two of them—the light brown and the smaller light green bear—were felted (causing them to shrink). The bear is constructed in two vertical halves (a leg and half the body) up to the shoulder, which, you should be forewarned, looks strange as you're working, and may cause you to wonder! After the two halves and the head are connected and stuffed (and the bear shape starts to look recognizable), the arms, head, nose, and ears are added. Face and paw details, which instantly give the bear its personality, are embroidered on when the bear is finished.

Because the bears don't need to be a particular size, you can skip the gauge swatch. Knit the first half of the body to the shoulder, then continue on if you like the way your work looks. If not, rip it out and start over. If your stitches are very tight, your bear may be stiffer and smaller than you initially intended. If your stitches are very loose, you can always felt the bear to tighten them up, provided you are using a yarn that felts. (Note: Cotton, linen, silk, synthetics, and machine-washable wool will not felt).

STITCH GUIDE

STOCKINETTE STITCH

ROW 1 AND ALL ODD-NUMBERED
   ROWS: Knit all sts.
ROW 2 AND ALL EVEN-NUMBERED
   ROWS: Purl all sts.

MAKE FIRST HALF OF BEAR FROM LEG TO SHOULDER

CO (cast on) 9 sts (stitches). Knit 1 row. Next row, WS (wrong side), inc (increase) 8 sts across by *P1, inc 1 using simple cast-on method (see page 52); repeat from * to last st, end p1—17 sts. Work on these 17 sts in St st (stockinette stitch) for 22 more rows, ending with a WS row—24 rows total.

SHAPE UPPER LEG

ROW 1: Knit to end of row, then increase 2 sts loosely using the simple cast-on method—19 sts.

ROW 2: Purl to end of row, then increase 2 sts loosely using the simple cast-on method—21 sts.

ROW 3: K2tog (knit 2 together; see page 53), knit to end of row—20 sts.

ROW 4: P2tog (purl 2 together), purl to end of row—19 sts.

ROWS 5 AND 6: Repeat Rows 3 and 4—17 sts after completing Row 6.

WORK BODY TO SHOULDER

Work 20 rows in St st on 17 sts, ending after you have completed a WS row.

Bind off for bear's shoulder as follows:

Next row (RS; right side): K6, BO (bind off) the next 8 sts, knit the last 3 sts—9 sts on right needle (5 before the BO section, and 4 after the BO section). Break yarn; place rem (remaining) 9 sts on an extra needle or holder. They will be combined with the stitches from the other side of the body to form the head, which will be worked in one piece.

Above: Both of these bears were made with Reynolds Lopi Icelandic wool. The one on the left was felted, making the fabric denser and the size smaller.

MAKE SECOND HALF OF BODY FROM LEG TO SHOULDER AND ATTACH TO FIRST HALF TO FORM NECK

Make the second side of the bear the same as the first side but after you finish the shoulder bind-off, do not break yarn. Instead, turn work and purl across 9 sts, then purl the 9 sts from holder—18 sts, with the BO sections poking out from the work like "kangaroo pouches."

MAKE HEAD

On the next RS row, *k1, inc 1 (using simple cast-on method); repeat from * across—36 sts. Work on these 36 sts for 5 rows, ending after you have completed a WS row. Beginning with the next RS row, shape head as follows:

ROW 1: *K5, k2tog; repeat from * to last st, end k1—31 sts.

ROW 2: Purl all sts.

ROW 3: *K4, k2tog; repeat from * to last st, end k1—26 sts.

ROW 4: Purl all sts.

ROW 5: *K3, k2tog; repeat from * to last st, end k1—21 sts.

ROW 6: Purl all sts.

ROW 7: *K2, k2tog; repeat from * to last st, end k1—16 sts.

ROW 8: Purl all sts.

ROW 9: K2tog to end of row—8 sts.

Break yarn and pull yarn tail tightly through rem sts like a drawstring.

SEW TWO SIDES OF BEAR TOGETHER

Using a yarn needle, sew the shoulders seams together invisibly using Bind Off to Bind Off mattress stitch (see page 23). Sew head, leg, and front and back seams using mattress stitch, as shown on page 45, leaving a 1" to 2" hole in the back for stuffing.

MAKE ARMS

CO 7 sts. Knit 1 row. On next row (WS), inc 6 sts across as follows: *P1, inc 1 (using simple cast-on method); repeat from * 5 more times, end p1—13 sts. Work on these 13 sts in St st for 17 rows. BO all sts. Make a second arm same as the first. Sew arm seams using mattress stitch.

MAKE EARS

CO 4 sts. Knit 1 row. On the next row (WS), inc 3 sts across as follows: *P1, inc 1 (using simple cast-on method); repeat from * 2 more times, end p1—7 sts. Work in St st for 2 rows. BO all sts. Make a second ear same as the first. Sew CO edge of each ear to side of head as shown in photograph, with the smooth (RS) of the fabric facing the front of the bear's head. Fold down the sides of each ear to form a shell-like shape and tack in place. The edges of the fabric will roll to the front to resemble the cupped shape of a bear's ear.

MAKE NOSE

CO 14 sts. Work in St st for 5 rows, beginning and ending with a purl row. On the next row (RS), k2tog to end of row—7 sts. Break yarn and pull through remaining sts like a drawstring to close the tip of the nose. Sew nose seam using mattress stitch.

FELT (OPTIONAL) AND STUFF

Weave in all ends. If you are felting the bear, place the bear body, arms, ears, and nose in a lingerie bag placed in a pillowcase. Tie the pillowcase closed tightly and felt according to the instructions for the baby tote on page 144.

After the felted pieces have dried, stuff the body and sew the stuffing hole closed. Stuff the arms and sew to the body. Stuff the nose and attach to the front of head as shown in photograph.

EMBROIDER FACE AND PAWS

Using satin stitch (see illustration at right), embroider the eyes and nose. Make mouth with open long stitches. Using open long stitches, make 4 long paw marks at ends of arms and legs. If you want to make the neck more distinct, run a piece of matching yarn in and out through all the neck sts, pull in slightly, tie at the back of the head, and weave in the ends.

BEAR
EMBROIDERY

SATIN STITCH

OPEN LONG STITCH

Satin stitch is commonly used in embroidery to fill in spaces, such as the bear's eyes and nose. An open long stitch is used for single lines, such as the bear's paws. Follow the illustration, and do not embroider so tightly that the fabric puckers. If you make a mistake, pull out the incorrect stitches one at a time, then resume working.

PARTY DRESS

SIZES

6 to 9 months, 9 to 12 months, 12 to 18 months, 18 to 24 months

Finished chest measurement: 21 (22$^1/_2$, 24$^1/_2$, 26)"

Shown in size 9 to 12 months

MATERIALS

1 skein Classic Elite Provence (125 grams/256 yards; 100% mercerized cotton) in rose garden #2655

1 pair size 6 straight needles, or size needed to obtain gauge

16-inch circular needle in size 6, or size needed to obtain gauge, for neckline finishing

$^1/_2$ yard 44" wide lightweight fabric, for skirt. Shown in duppioni silk.

Yarn needle

T-pins

Sewing thread to match skirt fabric

Sewing machine

GAUGE

18 sts and 32 rows = 4" on size 6 needles in seed stitch

This darling dress combines a quick-to-make knitted bodice with a simple sewn skirt. The neckline, armhole, and lower edge of the bodice are embellished with small bobbles, or decorative balls, directions for which are given in the Stitch Guide. The main part of the bodice features seed stitch and a subtle diamond border.

STITCH GUIDE

BOBBLED EDGE (over multiple of 8 stitches, plus 1):
ROW 1: (WS; wrong-side) *K4, (k1, p1, k1 into next st); turn work, p3, turn work, k3, pass 2nd and 3rd sts one at a time over the first st on right-hand needle to decrease the increased sts back to a single st to complete bobble; k3 (working the first st after the bobble tightly to avoid leaving a hole); repeat from * to last st, end k1.

SEED STITCH (over odd number of sts):
ALL ROWS: *K1, p1; repeat from * to last st, end k1.

DIAMOND BORDER: See chart.

CHOOSE SIZE

This pattern includes four sizes. The first number given refers to size 6 to 9 months, and the numbers in parentheses refer to sizes 9 to 12 months, 12 to 18 months, and 18 to 24 months, in that order. To make it easier to follow the instructions, choose the size you want to make and go through the pattern and highlight all of the numbers that apply to that size. If you do not want to write directly in the book, photocopy the instructions and highlight the copy.

MAKE GAUGE SWATCH

In order to be sure that the bodice will turn out the size you intend, take time to make a gauge swatch. Cast on 22 stitches and work in seed stitch for approximately 5 inches. Wash and block your swatch as you plan to wash the finished dress. Measure your gauge over a 4-inch-square section of the swatch, and adjust your needle size if necessary to obtain the correct gauge.

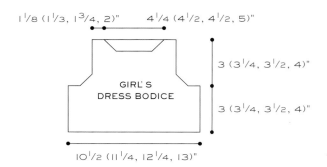

1 1/8 (1 1/3, 1 3/4, 2)"   4 1/4 (4 1/2, 4 1/2, 5)"

GIRL'S
DRESS BODICE

3 (3 1/4, 3 1/2, 4)"

3 (3 1/4, 3 1/2, 4)"

10 1/2 (11 1/4, 12 1/4, 13)"

MAKE BACK OF BODICE

CO (cast on) 49 (57, 65, 65) sts (stitches). Work row 1 of Bobbled Edge (see Stitch Guide on page 151) on first row, which is a WS row. Work the first 11 rows of the Diamond Border chart (see right). In Row 12 of chart, dec 2 (6, 10, 6) sts evenly across by knitting 2 sts together (see page 53) to give 47 (51, 55, 59) sts. Work in seed st until piece meas (measures) 3 (3 1/4, 3 1/2, 4)" from beginning, including bobbled edge. BO (bind off) 4 sts at beg of next 2 rows—39 (43, 47, 51) sts. BO 1 st at beg of next 10 rows—29 (33, 37, 41) sts. Continue in seed st without any further shaping until piece meas 6 (6 1/2, 7, 8)" from beginning, including bobbled edge. BO all sts.

MAKE FRONT OF BODICE

Work same as back until piece meas 4 1/2 (5, 5 1/2, 6 1/2)", from beginning, including bobbled edge, and end having just completed a WS (wrong side) row—29 (33, 37, 41) sts. Shape front neck as follows: Continuing in seed st, work 9 (10, 12, 15) sts (these will be the left shoulder stitches as the dress is worn), BO center 11 (13, 13, 11) sts, work rem (remaining) 9 (10, 12, 15) sts in pattern to end (these will be the right shoulder stitches as the dress is worn). At this point you will work only on the sts for the right shoulder. The sts for the left shoulder will stay on the needle, but you will ignore them for now. The BO sts at the center will provide enough separation between the two shoulders so you can work each independently. Working only on the sts for the right shoulder, where the yarn is connected, turn the work around and work 9 (10, 12, 15) sts in pattern. Turn again, BO 2 sts at the beginning of

the next RS row, work to end of row in pattern—7 (8, 10, 13) sts rem. Continue in this manner, working a WS row, then a RS row, binding off 2 sts at the beginning of each RS row, until there are 5 (6, 8, 9) sts rem for this shoulder. Work even (without any further shaping), until piece meas 6 (6 1/2, 7, 8)" from beginning, including bobbled edge. BO this group of sts. Now you will work on the sts for the other side. Join the working yarn to the neck edge of the left shoulder sts, ready to work a WS row. At the beginning of the next row, BO 2 sts, work in pattern to end—7 (8, 10, 13) sts. Turn again and work a RS row in pattern. Continue in this manner, working a WS row with 2 sts BO at the beginning, followed by a RS row, until 5 (6, 8, 9) sts rem. Work even until piece meas 6 (6 1/2, 7, 8)" from beginning, including bobbled edge. BO this group of sts. (As you have seen, because you can only BO sts at the beginning of a row, neck shaping is worked by BO sts at the beginning of RS rows for one side, and at the beginning of WS rows for the other side.)

FINISH NECKLINE

Using a yarn needle and the Bind Off to Bind Off mattress stitch (see page 23), sew shoulder seams. With circular needle and RS facing, beginning at left shoulder seam, pick up and knit 56 (64, 64, 72) sts evenly around neckline (see illustration on page 81) as follows: 10 (12, 12, 15) sts from left shoulder seam to beginning of front neck, 11 (13, 13, 11) sts from BO sts at front neck, 10 (12, 12, 15) sts from front neck to right shoulder seam, 25 (27, 27, 31) sts across back neck to left shoulder seam. Place marker after last stitch and join for working in the round (see page 100). Purl 1 round. Work bobbled BO on next round as follows: *BO 4 sts in purl st, (k1, p1, k1 into next st), turn work, k3, turn work, p3, pass 2nd and 3rd sts on right needle over first st on needle to decrease the increased sts back to 1 st and complete bobble, BO the bobbled stitch as if to purl, BO 3 more sts as if to purl; repeat from * to end of round to BO all sts.

FINISH ARMHOLES

With straight needles and RS facing, beginning at side edge, pick up and knit 49 (57, 57, 65) sts evenly around armhole as follows: 24 (28, 28, 32) sts to shoulder seam, 1 st in shoulder seam, 24 (28, 28, 32) sts to other side edge. Knit one row on the

DIAMOND BORDER

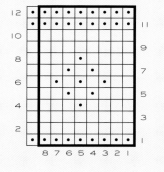

REPEAT OF 8 STS + 1,
AND 12 ROWS

KEY

☐ KNIT ON RS OF WORK,
PURL ON WS OF WORK

▣ PURL ON RS OF WORK,
KNIT ON WS OF WORK

TIPS FOR WORKING WITH THE CHART

This chart shows one repeat, plus an edge stitch. Work the chart from bottom to top. When you reach row 12, work decreases as explained in pattern.

ON RS (RIGHT-SIDE) ROWS: *Working from right to left, work the 8-stitch repeat (from stitch 1 to stitch 8) over and over until you reach the last stitch (the one outside the heavy outline repeat box), then work the last stitch.*

ON WS (WRONG-SIDE) ROWS: *Working from left to right, work the first stitch outside the repeat box once, then work the 8-stitch repeat (from stitch 8 to stitch 1) over and over until you reach the end of the row.*

WS. Work bobbled BO on next row as follows: BO 4 sts in purl st, (k1, p1, k1 into next st), turn work, k3, turn work, p3, pass 2nd and 3rd sts on right needle over first st on needle to decrease the increased sts back to 1 st and complete bobble, BO the bobbled stitch as if to purl, BO 3 more sts as if to purl; repeat from * to last st, BO last st as if to purl. Sew side seams using mattress stitch (see page 45). Block bodice to finished measurements (see page 24).

SEW SKIRT

Cut the skirt fabric to 12 (13 1/2, 15, 17)" x 42". Using a sewing machine, with right sides together, sew shorter sides together with a 5/8" seam allowance for center back seam. Sew 2 lines of machine-basting, 1/2" and 5/8" from one of the raw edges (this will be the waist). Evenly gather the fabric by pulling on the bobbin threads until the skirt fits the bottom edge of knitted bodice. Handstitch the bodice to the skirt. Hem skirt to desired length.

TODDLER MITTENS

SIZES

Toddler (up to 24 months)

MATERIALS

1 skein Mission Falls 1824 Wool (50 grams/85 yards; 100% machine-washable wool) in amethyst #23, denim #21, or poppy #11.

Small amount of contrasting color yarn, for embroidery (optional)

Yarn needle

IN-THE-ROUND METHOD
1 set of 4 size 5 double-pointed needles, or size needed to obtain gauge

1 set of 4 size 8 double-pointed needles, or size needed to obtain gauge

2 small stitch holders

3 stitch markers

BACK-AND-FORTH METHOD
1 pair size 5 straight needles, or size needed to obtain gauge

1 pair size 8 straight needles, or size needed to obtain gauge

2 medium stitch holders

2 stitch markers

GAUGE

4 1/2 stitches and 6 rows = 4 inches on size 8 needles in stockinette stitch

These mittens are sure to keep toddlers' hands toasty during cold weather. The floral or moon-and-stars embroidery is optional, as is the I-cord that connects the mittens and, ideally, keeps them together when it's run through the sleeves of a jacket. (Since the cord can be a choking hazard, only use when child is well supervised.) We give instructions for working these mittens in the round on double-pointed needles or back and forth on single-pointed needles. Choose the technique that you like best. Since this is such a small project, it is not necessary to knit a true gauge swatch. Instead, start knitting and after you have finished a few inches, measure your gauge. If it is correct, continue knitting. If it isn't, decide whether you want to start over with a different size needle, or accept that your mittens will be slightly larger or smaller than intended and continue.

IN-THE-ROUND METHOD

WORK CUFF

With smaller needles, loosely CO (cast on) 24 sts (stitches). Divide sts evenly on 3 needles, and join for working in the round, taking care not to twist the sts when joining (see page 101). Place a marker before the last stitch on the third needle to indicate the end of the round. Work in 1x1 rib for 1 1/2", increasing 1 st in last round of rib by kf&b (knit into the front and back of same stitch; see page 52)—25 sts. Change to larger needles and work in St st (stockinette stitch) for 4 rounds.

STITCH GUIDE

1 X 1 RIB:
(over even number of sts)
ALL ROUNDS: *K1, p1; repeat from * to end of round.

STOCKINETTE STITCH:
ALL ROUNDS: Knit all sts.

WORK THUMB GUSSET

ROUND 1: Work 11 sts, pm (place marker), kf&b, k1, kf&b, pm, work 11 sts to end—27 sts.

ROUND 2: Work all sts even without increasing.

ROUND 3: Work 11 sts, sl m (slip marker), kf&b, k3, kf&b, sl m, work 11 sts to end—29 sts.

MITTEN EMBROIDERY

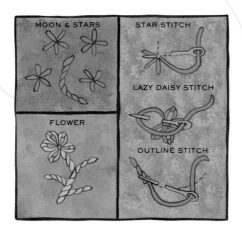

MOON & STARS

STAR STITCH

LAZY DAISY STITCH

FLOWER

OUTLINE STITCH

Shown here are the embroidery stitches for the toddler mittens. The moon is made with the outline stitch; the stars are made with the star stitch. The flower is made with the lazy daisy stitch. The leaves and stems are made with the outline stitch. Follow the illustrations, being careful not to embroider too tightly to avoid puckering the background fabric. If you make a mistake, remove the incorrect stitches one by one.

Repeat Rounds 2 and 3 as est (established), increasing 2 sts bet (between) markers every other round, until there are 9 sts bet the markers, making sure that you work every other round even (without increasing)—31 sts.

WORK HAND

Work 11 sts, remove first gusset marker, place the 9 thumb sts on a holder or yarn scrap to be completed later, remove second gusset marker, CO 4 sts across the gap using the simple cast-on method (see page 13), work 11 sts—26 sts. Work even on these 26 sts until mitten meas (measures) 3" above the 1 x 1 rib cuff, or 1" less than desired length.

DECREASE FOR TOP OF MITTEN

ROUND 1: *K2tog (knit 2 together; see page 53), k11; repeat from * one more time—24 sts.

ROUND 2: Work even.

ROUND 3: *K2, k2tog; repeat from * around—18 sts.

ROUND 4: Work even.

ROUND 5: *K1, k2tog; repeat from * around—12 sts.

ROUND 6: Work even.

ROUND 7: K2tog around—6 sts. Break yarn, leaving a 12" tail. Using a yarn needle, run end of yarn through rem (remaining) sts like a drawstring, and pull tight to close the top of the mitten.

WORK THUMB

Using larger needles, place the 9 sts from the holder on 2 needles, distributed as 4 on one needle and 5 on the other. With a 3rd needle and RS facing, join yarn to the beginning of the sts CO over the thumb gap. Pick up and knit 4 sts from the base of the CO sts, work across rem 9 sts to end. Join for working in the round—13 sts. Next round: K2tog, k9, k2 tog—11 sts. Repeat the previous round again—9 sts. Work even until thumb meas approximately 3/4" above pickup round. Decrease for top of thumb: K2tog 4 times, end k1—5 sts. Break yarn, leaving an 8" tail. Using a yarn needle, run end of yarn through rem sts like a drawstring, and pull tight to close the top of thumb. Weave in any loose ends. Make a second mitten the same as the first.

DECORATE WITH EMBROIDERY

Decorate back side of each mitten with floral or moon-and-stars embroidery shown in photograph on page 154 and in illustration at left.

MAKE CORD

CO 3 stitches and work a 36-inch I-cord (see page 64), leaving 12" tails at the beginning and end for attaching to mittens. Sew one end of the I-cord to the ribbing edge of each mitten, at the pinky finger side of the hand.

BACK-AND-FORTH METHOD

MAKE CUFF

With smaller needles, loosely CO
(cast on) 25 sts. Work in 1x1 rib for
1¹/2". Change to larger needles and
work in St st for 4 rows.

MAKE THUMB GUSSET

ROW 1: K11 sts, pm (place marker),
kf&b (knit into the front and back of
same stitch to increase 1; see page 52),
k1, kf&b, pm, k11—27 sts.
ROW 2: Purl all sts, sl m (slipping
markers).
ROW 3: Knit to first marker, sl m,
kf&b, knit to last st before the next
marker, kf&b, sl m, knit to end.
Repeat rows 2 and 3, increasing
2 sts bet (between) markers every
RS row, until there are 9 sts between
markers—31 sts. Purl one row.

WORK THUMB

On the next row, knit 11, remove
marker, slip 11 sts just worked to a
holder, k9 to second marker, remove
marker, and slip rem (remaining)
11 sts to another holder. Work on
9 thumb sts only until thumb meas
³/4" from the point where you started working the thumb separately,
ending having just completed a
WS row. Decrease for top of thumb
as follows:
ROW 1: K2tog (knit 2 together, see
page 53) 4 times, k1—5 sts.
ROW 2: P2tog 2 times, p1—3 sts.
Break yarn, leaving an 8" tail. Using
a yarn needle, run end of yarn
through rem sts like a drawstring,
and pull tight to close the top of
thumb. Sew thumb seam using the
mattress stitch.

WORK HAND

Slip 11 sts from first holder onto
right-hand needle. Join yarn at
thumb edge, and pick up and knit
4 sts from the base of the thumb,
slip 11 sts from 2nd holder onto left-
hand needle and knit them—26 sts.
Work even on 26 sts until mitten
measures 3" above 1 x 1 rib cuff or
1" less than desired total length. End
having just completed a WS row.
Decrease for top of hand as follows:
ROW 1: *K2, k2tog; repeat from * to
last 2 sts, end k2—20 sts.
ROW 2: Purl all sts.
ROW 3: *K1, k2tog; repeat from *
to last 2 sts, end k2—14 sts.
ROW 4: Purl all sts.
ROW 5: K2tog across—7 sts rem.
ROW 6: P2tog 3 times, end p1—
4 sts.
Break yarn, leaving a 12" tail.
Using a yarn needle, run end of yarn
through rem sts like a drawstring,
and pull tight to close the top of
the mitten. If you are not doing
embroidery, use a yarn needle, tail
of the yarn, and mattress stitch
(see page 45) to sew side seam from
wrist to top of hand. Weave in any
loose ends.

DECORATE WITH EMBROIDERY

Decorate the back side of each
mitten with floral or moon-and-stars
embroidery as shown in illustration
at left. After completing embroidery,
sew each side seam using the tail
of yarn and the mattress stitch, and
weave in any loose ends.

MAKE CORD

CO 3 stitches and work a 36-inch
I-cord (see page 64), leaving 12"
tails at the beginning and end for
attaching to mittens. Sew one end
of the I-cord to the ribbing edge of
each mitten, at the pinky finger side
of hand.

YARN SOURCES

For each project in this book, we have listed in the pattern the specific yarn we used. If you cannot find these yarns at your local yarn shop, we suggest that you contact the wholesale sources below and ask them to guide you to a retailer. If you would like to use a substitute yarn, choose one of very similar weight, yardage, and gauge, and, ideally, the same fiber content (all generally listed on the yarn label). Because fibers have different properties, they behave differently and will not necessarily yield comparable results. When buying more than one skein of a single color of yarn, make sure that all the skeins are from the same dyelot (that means they were dyed together and are an exact color match). The dyelot is printed on the yarn label, usually as a series of numbers and/or letters.

BROWN SHEEP COMPANY
100662 Cty. Rd. 16
Mitchell, NE 69357
800-826-9136
www.brownsheep.com.

CLASSIC ELITE YARNS
(JO SHARP)
12 Perkins St.
Lowell, MA 01854
800-444-5648
classicelite@aol.com

CRYSTAL PALACE YARNS
2320 Bissell Ave.
Richmond, CA 94804
510-237-9988
www.straw.com

DALE OF NORWAY
N16 W23390 Stoneridge Dr., Ste. A
Waukesha, WI 53188
800-441-3253
www.dale.no

GREEN MOUNTAIN SPINNERY
PO Box 568
Putney, VT 05346
800-321-9665
www.spinnery.com

JCA, INC. (REYNOLDS)
35 Scales Ln.
Towsend, MA 01469-1094
978-597-8794

JOSEPH GALLER
5 Mercury Ave.
Monroe, NY 10950-9736
800-836-3314

KOIGU WOOL DESIGNS
RR#1
Williamsford, Ontario
NOH 2V0, Canada
519-794-3066
www.koigu.com

LANE BORGOSESIA
527 Tejon S., Suite 200
Colorado Springs, CO 80903
719-635-4060

MANOS DEL URUGUAY
Design Source
PO Box 770
Medford, MA 02155
781-438-9631
shangold@aol.com

MUENCH YARNS, INC.
285 Bel Marin Keys Blvd., Unit J
Novato, CA 94949-5724
415-883-6375
muenchyarns@aol.com

RUSSI SALES, INC.
PO Box 4199
Bellingham, WA 98227
360-647-8289
www.russisales.com

UNIQUE KOLOURS, LTD.
(MISSION FALLS)
28 N. Bacton Hill Rd.
Malvern, PA 19355
800-25-2DYE4
www.uniquekolours.com

WESTMINSTER FIBERS
(JAEGER AND ROWAN)
5 Northern Blvd.
Amherst, NH 03031
603-886-5041
wfibers@aol.com

ACKNOWLEDGEMENTS

FROM KRISTIN & MELANIE

We started working on *Knitting for Baby* when our children were about two-and-a-half years old. We finished slightly less than a year later, a feat we could never have accomplished without our fabulous knitters who tested, knit, and sometimes reknit all of the projects. Thank you to Joyce Barnard, Kim Barnette, Niki Bronstein, Linda Brown, Peggy Desmond, Kim Estes, Gail Fulgham, Cynthia Frude, Mireille Holland, Alicia Hunsicker, Therese Inverso, Amy Johnson, Mary Langlois, Sam Maser, Esther Maynard, Susan Miles, Libby Mills, Carol Moran, Jeanne Moran, Dee Neer, Nancy Krom Nicholas, Laura O'Grady, Cathy Payson, Laurie Nicholas Rabe, Judy Scott, KeriAnne Shaw, Peggy Shuler, Louise Spangler, Diana Waill, Eva Westburg, Betsy Westman, Marion Wheaton, Susan Wheaton, and Claire Wilson.

We must heartily thank Ross Whitaker and his skilled and kind crew, who impressed us equally with their photographic talents and their love for babies. Our baby models were patient and sweet (as were their parents). Book designers Lynne Yeamans and Christine Licata melded together the text, photos, and illustrations to create the lovely pages before you. We are indebted to technical editor Lori Gayle, whose expertise, wit, and persnickety attention to detail is unique and invaluable, and to pattern-checker Dee Neer, whose vast experience in the technical field of knitting is overwhelming. We are grateful to all of the yarn companies that supplied us with materials, and to Linda Skolnik of Patternworks, who provided us with the tools on page 8 as well as her constant encouragement. The wind beneath our wings was our editor and publisher, Leslie Stoker, whose faith in what we could do kept us going even when we felt overwhelmed.

PERSONAL THANKS FROM KRISTIN

Cathy Payson has been more than a supportive friend. Her sharing and caring have enriched this book—and my life. Sally Lee has encouraged my creative endeavors in many of the decorative arts fields for many years. Linda Pratt has been a good friend, who continues to be supportive and encouraging as we travel through life on our sometimes converging paths. My friend and co-author Melanie Falick called me one evening, shortly after we had both had babies, with her vision for this book. Without her ideas and her faith in my creative abilities, this book would not have happened. Nathan Pratt became an invaluable studio assistant when the illustration deadline loomed. My mother, Nancy Krom Nicholas, constantly kept creative projects within my grasp while I was growing up and her mantra—"Make it yourself. It will mean more to you and will be an extra-special gift"— is still inspiring me. My dad, Arch Nicholas, and his mom, Frieda Roessler Nicholas, gave me my love of hard work. My husband, Mark Duprey, believes in what I do and has always been there for me with his gentle manner, support, encouragement, and love. My daughter, Julia Nicholas Duprey, brightens my days and nights with enthusiasm and gives her father and me hope for the future.

PERSONAL THANKS FROM MELANIE

I feel honored to co-author a book with Kristin Nicholas and thank her for devoting herself so whole-heartily to it. It is her creative brilliance that makes it shine. I could never have done my part without the support of my mom, Diana Waill, and my husband, Christopher Whipple. My father, Howard Falick, has shared his love of beauty with me for my entire life and in this way has greatly influenced both my work and home life. Linda Ligon, owner of Interweave Press, understood this project was important to me and allowed me to take it on even though she knew it could distract me from my job as editor of her magazine, *Interweave Knits*. Ann Budd, my coworker and friend, kept the magazine moving forward when the distractions proved true. And when the weight of it all proved too heavy, the staff at Trapeze School taught me how to fly. And finally, and most importantly, there is my son, Ben, who helped me to keep the work in perspective and brings more joy into my life than I ever dreamed possible.

INDEX